Dark Lullaby

I write with the idea of a human being in front of me and what I want to tell him.

Milton Acorn

Dark Lullaby

the winning poems
of the 2000
Sandburg-Livesay Anthology
Contest

judged by
Robert Sward

UnMon America
Pittsburgh, 2004

Poems copyright © the authors, 2004
This collection copyright © Unfinished Monument Press, 2004
Cover and frontispiece illustrations copyright © Gilda Mekler, 2004
All rights reserved

Library of Congress Cataloging-in-Publication Data

Dark lullaby : the winning poems of the 2000 Sandburg-Livesay
Anthology Contest / judged by Robert Sward.
        p. cm.
    ISBN 1-884206-10-7
    1. Canadian poetry — 20th century. 2. American poetry —
20th century. 3. English poetry — 20th century.
    I. Sward, Robert, 1933- II. Sandburg-Livesay Anthology
Contest (2000)

PR9195.7.D37 2004
811'.54080971 — dc22   2004057221

UnMon America

(a division of Unfinished Monument Press)
PO Box 4279
Pittsburgh, PA
15203 - 0279

Unfinished Monument Press is a subsidiary of
Mekler & Deahl, Publishers

Cover and frontispiece illustrations: Gilda Mekler
Design by Gilda Mekler
Printing by Transcontinental
Printed in Canada

Table of Contents

Liliane Welch, Tattoo 2
    Household Tools 3
    Portage 4
    Sex 5
Roger Bell, I'm only fourteen 6
    Baby born in a toilet 7
    Shelby Springs Confederate Cemetery 9
Marilyn Gear Pilling, After Watching Red, White and Blue 10
Gina Riley, Bugbear 11
Rina Ferrarelli, Y M Lee 12
    On the Outer Banks 13
Linda Frank, You've Been On My Mind 14
    Turquoise 15
    November Rain 16
    36°C 17
    Mercy 18
Becky D. Alexander, In a Cornfield 20
Kristin Andrychuk, The Harvest 21
    Afterwards 22
Tammy Armstrong, Lines of Body 23
    Carol 26
Winona Baker, The Children of the Man in the Moon 27
David Barnett, Half-Brothers 29
Jacqueline Bartlett, Poor Tommy Shop 30
Theda Bassett, Beyond What the Eyes See 31
Catherine Bayne, The Elm 32
Marion Beck, Pruning 33
Patricia M. Benedict, 6 haiku 34
Paul Berry, Remembering on GNER 36
Izak Bouwer, 2 haiku 37
Ronnie R. Brown, Pas de Deux 38
    Family Ties 40
    The Scent of Love 42
    Background Shadow 44
Brian Burke, the harvest tree 45
Anita Gevaudan Byerly, Fourth and Hawkins — April, 1944 46
Terry Ann Carter, Meeting the Novelist at a Cocktail Party 47
Denise Coney, haiku 48
Gloe Cormie, By the River on Opening Night 49
Terrance Cox, Armstrong's Cornet 50
Barbara Ruth Crupi, Last Lines: The Letter 51

Ernest Dewhurst,	Echoes of a Shot Firer	53
	Teacher Aunt	55
John Dixon,	Moorside	57
Fay Eagle,	Lot 109: Fanscape of a Victorian Lady	58
Gerald England,	Under Macgillycuddy's Reeks	59
Janice M. Faria,	Magician	60
Michael Fraser,	Separation	61
Ann Goldring,	2 haiku	62
Alistair Halden,	The Other Scotland	63
Irene Blair Honeycutt,	Stroupie in Autumn	64
Sheila Hyland,	Moonlight	65
Ellen S. Jaffe,	Night of My Conception: Ellen's Story	66
	Chaco Canyon — Revisited	68
Hans Jongman,	Coffee	69
Kristine Kaposy,	haying in	70
Earl R. Keener,	Lanterns	71
Philomene Kocher,	haiku	72
Ken Kowal,	after the festival	73
David P. Kozinski,	Magic	74
Joan Latchford,	Tank	75
John B. Lee,	The Chair of Angels	76
	Red Barns	78
	Walking Along Lake Erie	80
	Paying Attention	83
Anne Lewis-Smith,	Little Haven at Low Tide	86
	Dun Aonghasa, Aran	88
Noah Leznoff,	pushing in the grocery line	89
Robert Lima,	After an Anonymous Eighth-Century Gaelic Poet	90
Norma West Linder,	Sonnet for Martha	91
Mikal Lofgren,	Winter Touching the Bones	92
Robin Lovell,	2 haiku	93
Neil mac Neil,	Sow the Good Seed	94
Giovanni Malito,	Sarnia, Ontario, 1981	96
Joy Hewitt Mann,	It is the moon	97
	What Nobody Knows About Spring at the Seniors' Home	99
John E. Marks,	Working Girl	101
Ben Murray,	First Night	102
Sue Nevill,	Mother/daughter/portrait	103
	azimuths	104
Renee Norman,	My Father, Driving	105
H.F. Noyes,	3 haiku	107
Anne-Marie Oomen,	Ode to Dirt in an Old Farmer's Lungs	108
Kathy Pearce-Lewis,	Aubade	110
Linda Vigen Phillips,	Dress Rehearsal	111
Peggy Poole,	Fête de la Musique, Geneva	112

Al Purdy, *House Guest*	113
Lynn Veach Sadler, *As Silent as Mimes*	116
Joanna Catherine Scott, *What Time Does*	118
Jeff Seffinga, *Spring's First Crop*	119
Shirley A. Serviss, *Sowing words*	121
K.V. Skene, *In Like a Lion*	122
Tammara Or Slilat, *Atonement Day*	123
Marvin Smith, *Visiting Ray Chapman's Grave*	124
Raymond Souster, *Love Birds*	125
While the Smog Burns Off	126
The Bird Who Somehow Could Not Fly	127
Margaret Speak, *Set to Last*	128
Elizabeth St Jacques, *Points of Light*	130
Sandra Staas, *Turning the Coals*	132
Jean Stanbury, *Tribute*	133
Valerie Stetson, *Wedding Story Love*	134
Sheila Stewart, *Ladybones*	135
Andrew Stickland, *A Midsummer-Night's Lament*	136
Lynn Tait, *Mother and Son*	137
Adèle Kearns Thomas, *Runaway*	138
Carolyn Thomas, *2 short poems*	139
Stephen Threlkeld, *Good-morning*	140
Mildred Tremblay, *Codeine and Roses*	141
Lilka Trzcinska-Croydon, *Sorrow*	142
Mourning	144
Sandee Gertz Umbach, *The Bra Factory*	145
'Panasomu' People	147
Wendy Visser, *haiku*	149
f.ward, *in spite of all those taxes*	150
Patricia Wellingham-Jones, *Flatlanders Head for the Hills*	153
A.Z. Wells, *From Suffering into Laughter*	154
Joanna M. Weston, *tanka*	155
Patience Wheatley, *In an Old Limestone House at Belleville*	156
Sheila Windsor, *haiku sequence*	157
haiku sequence	158
Elana Wolff, *The Way to Make a Mask*	159
Margaret Malloch Zielinski, *Mallory*	160
Lizzie	162
Notes on the Poets	163
Robert Sward — Final Judge	179
Bernadette Rule — Preliminary Judge	180
Acknowledgements	181
About Carl Sandburg & Dorothy Livesay	184

Liliane Welch

First Prize

Tattoo

After the war she could live
only *Auschwitz*, sitting with relatives
in their sunlit kitchen, her immortal
rock. And when she ate the chocolate
cake and picked up all the crumbs,
it was always *Auschwitz*, a new disbelief,
maybe, or the cell blocks now
bolted, like the soot sky,
the tiered bunks a watermark
left intact inside her head. Each sip
of coffee in the china cup,
a fresh flow of grief
she'd shouldered, had been
miraculously freed from, but now
it was everything, the dress
she pulled tight around her hips,
black comb in her hair, nephews
when they turned cartwheels,
all cast down the mass grave
of that word. And in dreams
she sang it, dark lullaby
as she strained
to wake, cradling,
her tattooed arm
like a lost child.

Household Tools

The 1996 Johannes Vermeer Exposition

We walk into these
    paintings, an intimate
little street, through passageways
    the inner courtyards
of quotidian concerns.

Stories sealed
    by the hourglass
of silence. How intense
    their lives are,
resonant, serene. This figure,

Vermeer's milkmaid, raising
    her red arms
over odour of bread,
    to pour milk.
Let's prolong that light.

The century of discovery.
    A woman gazing into her
mirror, a writer
    transfixing her viewer,
a geographer searching the outside.

Faces charged by bridled desire.
    Can we grow those eyes?
And the milk keeps flowing from
    strong hands, stained as sunsets,
handling household tools, making
    everything possible.

Portage

When March wind rides on the body
and the heart tears skin from trees,
you and I struggle through a portage, slip
into the river below the falls and paddle —
move faster than the banks,
out of the thickets in our heads.
Dense bush protects from forbidden reaches.

We feed the fire with sticks before sleep,
that the water might
carry us on. But only

the rapids roil through the night, a cello
full of oceans and lakes, so deep
so adventurous we become again
cartographers who draw

new maps and dream.
We must break free, reach those shores, deliver
the pine stumps, rocks, bogs
that return now faster every March.

Sex

> *Memory is a strange Bell —*
> *Jubilee, and Knell.*
> — Emily Dickinson

His father's voice and a woman's laughter sounded through
The closed bedroom door; the radio played; it was August.
And (of that love-talk) some mysterious story
Engulfed for years the neatly-made parental bed.

At mealtime, given body, it became
The secret, hot afternoon he and
His brother practiced forgetting — while
Their mother blessed and served the meat.

And this was her trade, that forgiving wife
Who disappeared behind a pink apron
Avoiding the small catastrophes of betrayal
Endlessly through respectable talk,

The safety of sewing circle and church.

Roger Bell

SECOND PRIZE

I'm only fourteen

*to those who died
and those who did their best to save them*

Show me God or one good thing
any laughter hidden behind a shy fan of hands
any sleepover secrets
anything girlish and giddy
about tortured steel and flame
people trying to extinguish screams
within the jealous push away of heat
and smoke that closes around her
like a blanket pulled up by
some parent before bed, checking his children.

This is not Jeanne d'Arc
the willing bride of fire
this girl didn't seek this out
she has no cause
all she has is fourteen years
and begging
one day more

but she is softened to silence
and ashes drifting down.

Those who tried to help turn weeping away
her echo still clutching at their hollowed hearts   later
lift their heads
to the cruel glitter
the false promise
of the not so distant horizon
where sun grandiosely sweeps away the fog.

Baby born in a toilet

The little girl
grunted out and left
in the bus station toilet
survived   will become
a distance swimmer
cross the English Channel twice
and Lake Ontario
then try the North Atlantic

she wants cold waters
so her mind numbs
but her body remembers
the chubby legs and arms
beating
in those first porcelain hours

she'll swim, will refuse all help
          will refuse the refuge
of warm drinks
and kind wishes
will shake off eels and tides
limbs moving against death
remembering the loose tether
of the umbilicus
the shock of entry
the eyes opening
to a hard world

she is swimming
    is swimming
against night
against fatigue
against the desire to desist
and settle to the seabed

cheer her on, little orphan girl
flailing against namelessness
              injustice
              desertion
across the tilting water
almost there
cheer her on
into harbour
then the shallows
first few shaky steps
on the uncertain bottom
then
a big breath and
ashore

Shelby Springs Confederate Cemetery

Elias Early
Co. G
28 Ala. Inf.
Apr. 18, 1862

I have been here so long
this red soil has about rubbed me away.
My children, their children too, are done
their atoms slowly peregrinating towards me.
One far day there will be a reunion of Earlys
our rebel bones ground to dust
our last uneasy cries transmogrified
by mockingbirds and made music.

Ma always said, *Elias*
your name is like a sigh.
Now listen, listen to the tall pines
like mothers
exhaling a time-tempered regret
over these two hundred and seventy-seven graves.

Marilyn Gear Pilling

THIRD PRIZE

After Watching Red, White *and* Blue

Every evening of that week I watched a film
set in France
and by the end of the week I wanted to take up
smoking.
All the women smoked.
All had long legs, chic haircuts, smart shoes, purses
of soft leather that swung from one
shoulder, purses that held the knowledge
of what it was to be Woman, the props
for a life where sex filled
all the interstices.
With eyes that burned I watched
how those women opened
their purses, felt
for the package, tapped
the cigarette from its place in the row
of identical brothers.
I watched the curve
of their wrists as they flicked
on fire, the quick dip
of their heads as tip touched flame.
The concentration of the first inhalation.
How then the burdens of their foreheads and necks
and shoulders loosened and rolled away,
how with the second in-breath their eyes went un-
seeing and they curled themselves
for reverie.
Those women.
I want their legs, their haircuts, their sex lives,
the secrets of their purses, but mostly I want
those islands in their lives
where the smoke drifts effortlessly beyond their fingers and
out of time.

Gina Riley

HONOURABLE MENTION

Bugbear

Survival ensured nothing was ever wasted —
After eighteen thousand years
a flute is found
hollowed from the bone of a bear.

So music has one root
in sucking bone, belching
           by a wood-fire
old red jumper of thick-skinned fur.
Music began flowing
from the wounding order of the hunt
the sheepishness of fireside predators.
Sparring with a thousand pounds of muscle
teeth and claw, only the fittest
could conceive a catchy tune
fingers that would shape a flute, survival
of the sweetest
above the moaning of a honey bear.

You and I prefer its tender heights
listening in the living room
      wolf moon golden
       great Bear beautiful
on a summer night.
How light-heartedly we make our home
love each other in a wilderness
harmony
no less hazardous than before.
Until we come to mourn
the sound of passing tenderness
tomorrow's silent aeons
doubt, old bugbear of our own.
Only the fittest
only the fittest can believe
    nothing is ever wasted.
They feel it in their bones.

Rina Ferrarelli

Honourable Mention

Y M Lee

Through the haze of another
Monday morning   the trolley glass
and Chinese laundry window
I see him leaning on his elbows
next to a vase of purple mums
white collar and cuff
cardigan pewter like his clipped
well-brushed hair   Y M Lee
who puts everything
through the mangle
linen tablecloths
and jeans with snaps
who reckons in the old way
Chinese?   American?
everything comes out the same
on his abacus   he bends forward
hands clasped as if in prayer
ready to start again
at the beginning.

On the Outer Banks

To the Wright Brothers

And life sometimes is on the fringes
a fringe of sandbanks strung along the coast
what a relief there is made by human hands
shapes of work   shapes of leisure

blending with the pebbles and coarse brown sand
you plover your way in and out
constant motion one way to survive

or you forget about all that:
singleminded about your needs
you incubate your dream in a drafty barn
until it grows wings
then watch it rise above the low landscape
soar higher than gull and sea hawk.

Linda Frank

Honourable Mention

You've Been On My Mind

> *I'm just whispering to myself, I can't pretend*
> *That I don't know*
> — Bob Dylan

Perhaps it's the fate of the yellow
chrysanthemum so arresting
in my October garden
that places you
here on my mind
when I will not place you
in my life

Or the shock of yellow flowers
I've gathered for my windowsill
that tells me
how I can not
gather your body
in my arms
Maybe it's the mark of yellow
dust from anthers
pregnant with pollen
staining my fingertips
that reminds me of how
I will not allow
my hands
to touch you

This yellow
arrived so late
in my fall garden
This yellow
bursting
from darkness

Turquoise

I am not fooled by doves
who sit still as statues under the moon
mute witness to the desire
that clamours for you
like a flock of wild birds raging
the blue-rimmed eyes of doves
that stare empty
at the aching
poems you hold out to me
like a bird's egg
in the palm of your hand

I watch doves fly
under a February moon
that hauls itself whole
into the smoky augural sky
And all the winter birds
hold their silence
when you turn from me
and walk away, leaving
only empty nests
etched naked and cold
across that lonely Boston moon

I hold my breath
try to silence
the frantic beating of wings
in the shadows of my heart
I still can't say your name
and this much has not changed between us
I have nothing to give
Only this turquoise
this fragile song I've held for so long
like a bird's egg
in the warmth of my mouth

November Rain

> *Even the blackbirds broke veins in their hearts*
> *singing love songs*
> — **Sandra Alcosser**

This is my heart
startled
like the sudden flight
of a thousand black
birds flung to the air
as a flock of leaves
the tree throws off
in a fright
of adrenaline

This is my heart
scattered
like the panic of black
birds in wild disarray
confused by the weather
not knowing
if they should fly
south or try
to last out
the winter

This is my heart
buried
deep in a blanket of black
birds settled uneasily
over the bare limbs
of a November tree
ready to fly
at any change
in the wind

36ºC

If it weren't for the northern trees
oak and white pine forest
out behind the cottage,
you'd think we were deep
in the cotton belt
of Georgia or South Carolina
on the back roads of Kentucky
Our cabin so ramshackle
we sit like a cliché
in all those movies about the south,
out on the screened-in porch
rocking the rotting floor boards
under the slow swing of the fan
lemonade vapour breath
in the blistering heat
The air so still
even the gulls can't find
a current to ride
and each listless leaf
sounds a storm
in the hollow
of our ears

Mercy

It happened for the first time
in Arizona one Easter
Jesus cried
out to her, his eyes deep
in exquisite agony
a thin film of sweat
like a sheen icing his body
his hair tangled to his shoulders
The pulsing force of him
shot up her pelvis
to the very palms of her hands

He spoke to her
many times since then
He'd whisper secrets of the desert
in her ear when she bent
to him, wetting his lips
with her tongue. She retied
his hands to the cross
She stroked their bodies. His hard
alabaster muscles, her own
soft thighs
Jesus was so good looking
She'd meet him everywhere
descended from the cross
wearing sandals and ripped blue jeans
open flannel shirts, his hair long
and a ring piercing his ear
She found him cross-legged and blissful
in city parks, slouched and pouting
against downtown graffiti walls
He beckoned her from hidden doorways
in dusty Phoenix streets
tormented her, testing her love

She wore a crown of thorns
and wandered in graveyards west of Phoenix. With arms
outstretched, she healed each cactus
with the heat of her body
and the touch of her hands
She licked his blooddrops
leaking from her open palms
Men betrayed her
with each kiss

When he visits her now
she comes like angels
then flies away

Becky D. Alexander

In a Cornfield

Farmers say you can hear the corn grow.
Here in this field
      under the blind of rising sun
      under a sky streaked with white
two eagles float on air
suspended in the deep blue . . .
no flapping of wings
silent spirals up and down,
      around in the currents
      of wind and heat.

The sound of water
trickling down a forest stream —
      the water a mirage
      here in this crisp field.

Spring in the cornfield . . .
crumpled stubble bent and dry . . .
      fodder for the wind.

Corn not growing,
but remembering
      its other voices.

Kristin Andrychuk

The Harvest

Beyond the screen
bees harvest
windfall pears
while I kiss
each knob of your spine
hard bones
soft inner thighs
over-ripe pears'
slight perfume
is replaced
by your sweeter musk.
The bees and I
burrow and suck
and the air vibrates
humming through our bodies.
Bees tunnel pears
while we harvest.

Afterwards

The leaves lie heaped brown mounds
The limbs are bare
No more green fans orchid blooms
The grey wood creaks
on this cold day

Seed pods shrivel unopened
on frozen ground
The screens are stored for winter
but you and I sit on the veranda

We watch the wind
tear down the last few leaves

The cold makes us both shiver
but we stay
looking for something
some message from this day

I look in your eyes
then away
No need for speech

The dark swaying branches
the wind scattering brown leaves
Dry as dust leaves
fragmented

Tammy Armstrong

Lines of Body

I

Beer, cedar snapping fire now
      in your cottage:
decades of family,
the antique Wedgewood,
river stone chimney,
      tilting always to the north.
My cigarettes fill the ear of a scallop shell
placed among inglenook trinkets
while you top drinks, hum along to Dave Brubeck.

II

A mile between,
      there are no neighbours at the edge of the island,
but freedom,
here in the bed
      as hearth fire grumbles, eats and growls.
We've know each other one day
but will wake into washed-out light,
      legs entangled,
your lips to my forehead
as though it's always been.

III

      This carapace of
an unspeakable affair,
      shunned outside doors:
exiled lovers,
traipsing the island bowl,
      together beautiful —
a stone in your hand.

IV

        At night, we walk the shores,
over log boom loss,
our ankles slipping easily
between creosote land wash,
        where East meets West you say —
Georgia Strait wrapping
        around the shattered edge of an oxbow inlet.

V

I have spent years roaming back
        to the ocean
until here with you,
hands slick on ice stones,
I'm tethered
        to our salt-glazed perceptions.

VI

Something here,
        something a vocabulary, a lexicon will destroy,
the spell shattered —
you, suddenly
a pale stranger, tattoo at your shoulder,
our lips raw, tattered where they ran
        along the lines of body.

VII

Morning sky hyacinth,
rusty along the horizon,
where an eaglet skates near the point,
    over ice brash, damask waves,
fish in talons, surface skimming.
It storms up through the rains, into flatwoods —
    a ling cod carrying through
this timeless winter.

VIII

Cabins have burnt during blizzards,
the flames euphoric as they gnash pale sky,
    edge back the snow line
as I do each time my tongue traces your neck
    and you whisper, *yes* —
        such elements never survive together long.
smoldering, exhausted when light is finally revived.
    We never intended to love well.

Carol

Evenings with the push-pedal Singer
sewing sofa covers, throw pillows in gaudy baroque print,
the threads broke rashes on your fingers and arms.
Mornings — a freedom of picking at five dollars a bushel,
months spent reaching into autumn
into the flames of apple and cloud.

I grew taller.
By twelve,
spent too many hours on the vanity,
feet in sink, mooning over adolescent reflections.
There will always be more beautiful women, you said,
as I rested my chin on your pippin-scented hair,
stepped on your shoes, so foolish,
more childlike than my own.

Those nights while father complained
of watered whiskey, the cost of family,
you studied to have grade twelve before us
but sister grew into angry gristle
and you and I learned to smoke together,
how to leave men on rainy afternoons.
We never went out for milk
but to other provinces, other countries.
Drunk, I found myself calling you
from a Budapest brothel,
while German school boys took my picture.

But those mornings
when apples froze in the kill frost,
no one needed new chesterfield prints,
you performed puppet shows with scrap-box pleats,
your face perhaps darkened, a jaw slightly swollen —
our world, tight, but with beauty,
your beauty as you threaded a silver needle,
sutured a button eye back into place.

Winona Baker

The Children of the Man in the Moon

The children of
the man in the moon
are close to their mother
Their father goes off
as soon as he finds
she's pregnant
again

The children have eyes
like Orphan Annie's
Go to school
as required   leave
as soon as they're able
At recess they huddle
    watching the way
    children play

Live on a farm
mostly woods   has sea frontage
Their dogs
descended from wolves
The children of
the man in the moon
have eyes like their father

Long-haired and
barefoot in summer
they come to town
with berries and baskets
cascara bark
driftwood and oysters
all kinds of mushrooms

➤

Don't know what religion
they follow   if any
Sometimes hear singing
more of a chant

Why do that
they don't bother us

The children of
the man in the moon
don't know their father

David Barnett

Half-Brothers

In Nevern churchyard a yew
bleeds even yet.
Though a branch was lopped
off. (Cursed surgery.)
Its blood seeps. Womanly.
Matting a round of magpie-
dances below a copestone.
Priestesses with their craft
to yolk more kindly
issue for their race.

Men merely mime
the squat, spread, press
through the soul's pipe.
Since their blood's stuck
to their harrow-fret.
Scythe arms. Breasts
pressed against a column.

And to their heads' trenches.
To strain it they gush
the blood of others. Crossing
swallows. Cree. Gypsies
in their tents. Hounded
otters. Harvest mice.

Near this yew's a Celtic
cross. Taller than
an axe-handle. Its knots
make up a code.
From a shocked god.

Jacqueline Bartlett

Poor Tommy Shop

When she said "Lakeland"
I saw you walking the slopes
of the saw-toothed hills
between Beckside and Lindale
arriving before dawn
for a bowl of porridge
too hot to eat.

In the rimed yard
among clattering buckets
skimmed with ice
you saw the red sun
barely strike the fells
felt the gripe of hunger
in your gut.

When she said "Lakeland"
there you were in the must of the hen-house
foraging for eggs
letting the slime of yolk and albumen
slip down your throat
from the blown shell.

Years later
in the room at your niece's house
a thin cupboard
hoarded rinds of bread
biscuits, wrinkled fruit
among the shirts and socks
you stacked carefully
as a dry-stone wall.

Before the First World War *Poor Tommy Shop* was a term used by Lakelanders to describe a workplace where food was in short supply.

Theda Bassett

Beyond What the Eyes See

Music of Edvard Grieg stirs me all day.
Above fjords, mists cling to mountain rows.
The country roads repeat like his rondos,
each switchback curve becomes a roundelay.
The craggy rocks, the beech and pine replay
in leaf-green forests like adagios.
The waterfalls crash wild fortissimos.
I want to be a summer stowaway,
engulf myself in grandeur that appeals.
The forest scenes in Norway do intrigue
with mountains, mists, fjords and cloud-lined skies.
I sense the reverence each Norwegian feels.
Small wonder that music of Edvard Grieg
conveys a beauty hard to verbalize.

Catherine Bayne

The Elm

grey weathered
wraith of a tree,
life drawn down
to the weight of a single leaf
trembling from the breath
of a swallow's passing,
branches spiraling to sky
in a grace of motion,
dancing into death
as few dance
in their living

Marion Beck

Pruning

The last day in October
bright with sun
tempts me out
              in the garden
the green ash stripped of leaves
reveals black branches
intertwined and crossing
they scarify with the lightest air

it must be pruned
and staring at the mesh
considering what must go
what stay
I realize how difficult
the first cut is

Patricia M. Benedict

Busy washday —
The kitchen reeks of bleach,
Left-over meat and peas.

Graveyard wind —
Father's tears drown the flowers
On Mother's grave.

On the outhouse door —
Silvered by the setting sun
A spider's web.

Rivered streets —
Barefoot children at play
among the hailstones.

Snow-flecked awning —
Summer dresses — shivering,
On Sale.

How is my dog to know
she is chasing the last of
the Summer wind?

Paul Berry

Remembering on GNER

After warnings a whistle starts them:
train journeys and troops over the top
and Great North Eastern's remembrance.
Piped shrill through carriage speakers,
silence, marshalled, comes to attention.
November's poppies parade on lapels,
or mastheads of *Sun* and *Times*.

Along the Flying Scotsman's route
bomber country's rain-glazed fields:
a season or troop movement away
from winter wheat or Flanders mud.
Ruined runways and pillboxes pass,
skeletal trees guard headlands,
propane mortars defend seedbeds.

Enter a tunnel: remembrance spoils
for want of visual clues or popping ears.
Landscapes remind longer with traces,
signs men mark then move away from.
At Grantham the guard says time is up,
gives corporate thanks and reminds York
next stop, lest by remembering we forget.

GNER: Great North Eastern Railway, linking London with Scotland

Izak Bouwer

October fog
cannot hide
the maples

autumn evening
birch and its leaves
by the street lamp

Ronnie R. Brown

Pas de Deux

Do not tell me of the finger
entering that elegant throat;
of muscles that ache, bones
that creak. I do not wish
to speak of the fact
that he, of the firm behind,
the promising
crotch, watches
with longing
the boys
in the *corps de ballet*.

Please, don't say
that they are
sore, strained,
constantly in pain. As he lifts her
high—his hand
secure on her taut inner thigh—
I want only to look,
see beauty,
truths—
sex, death, birth,
life—there
for me
in the studied movements
of the dance.

As a child
I loved the homes
in the better parts of town. Pure,
white curtains blew in the summer breeze.
I stared into those windows
and I knew
the joy, the ease,
the life that chosen people lived.

Now, on the stage,
I watch—each step
a promise offered up to me.
Don't even ask,
I know
I don't care to see
those things that happen
when the curtains
close.

Family Ties

While her grandmother's mind
slipped away,
her mother and aunts
argued, debating where
the old woman should go
and when and how. Hours
spent on long-distance
conversation. Hours
in which each recreated
history.

The only thing
on which they could agree
was the making of a memory album,
expensive, leather-bound,
they purchased it
as a group,
each claiming so many pages
choosing photos, mementos,
present and past
to try and fix their place
in their mother's waning memory.

When she died
they descended as one
each anxious
to take back her share.

They beamed
as the social worker
spoke of how their mother had carried it
everywhere, pointing to picture
after picture long after she'd lost
interest in nearly everything
else. Pointing
even after her power
of speech was gone.

But the album that was given back
was tattered paper,
cheap, filled
with the images of strangers.

It took more than a month
for the staff
to track their album down
and hours of patient coaxing
before the social worker
could pry it free
from the arms
of another old woman
who kept insisting
the people within
belonged
to her.

The Scent of Love

for Ellen

You wanted their pasts
to be better than your own, worked
so they might have perfect
childhood memories.

You stayed at home;
refused to entrust them
to the care of strangers; did
special little things
in the hope that they
would remember.

You tell me of the bread you baked,
one of many daily tasks undertaken
for the sake of the kids.
Three tiny children lifted
to the kitchen counter
each with their own
small ball of dough, kneading,
kneading. The first time
they saw store-bought loaves
they had to ask you
what they were.

Now, all this
is forgotten
your children remembering only
that back then
you wore a pony tail,
were *there*.

What can I tell you?
Only that sometimes
taking sheets down
from the line
I'll press them to my face
and thoughts of my mother
flood back.
Or walking down a street
I'll catch a whiff
of Spearmint gum
and, in an instant, be
my daddy's little girl.

These moments wait
for your children, too.
One day
they'll smell
the fragrance you wear,
the scent from your garden or,
perhaps, the aroma
of fresh-baked bread

and, for a moment
they will remember
love.

Background Shadow

Behind me
cool, cool
lips on the nape
of a summer's evening
leaning toward night
leaning, tongue
delicately licking salt
from the rim
of collar bone
unexpected,
a secret
Valentine in the mail,
     kiss
under mistletoe.
Behind me
and I could be
anyone — female, male, all
lovers — anything
readied, positioned to
leapfrog, hearts
bolting like a Greyhound
bus revving up, shifting into me
and I could be
anywhere, years
from that breath
so hot on my back
porch, so hot
I cannot
leave it
behind.

Brian Burke

the harvest tree

branches stiff as winter tines
a live frozen thresher for tossing winter wheat
no scarf of snow yet
no shawl of white for warmth

if hoar frost harvests were possible
each tree would sift its weight in husk & chaff
separate fragile bract & fodder
would rake the frigid air
nature sowing an unexpected yield
of alien crops   fourth season

winter wheat
wind-driven through bare thresher trees
rime-harsh   near lifeless
but swaying   swaying

Anita Gevaudan Byerly

Fourth and Hawkins — April, 1944

At the corner of Fourth and Hawkins
was Bonomo's fruit market,
where I once found a pen pal
in a basket of strawberries,
and Jackson's drug store,
where I worked after school
and weekends for $12.00 a week
Next to the bowling alley
was Felder's Bar and my dad
spent too many nights there
unwinding after double shifts
at the Edgar Thomson steel mill.
At home, mother counted ration coupons
and I longed for real silk stockings.
It was April, 1944, two months
before the invasion of Normandy...
Auschwitz and Hiroshima
places unknown.

Terry Ann Carter

Meeting the Novelist at a Cocktail Party

I wonder what it must be like
to be you, to turn words
into flesh in the small towns
of your imagination

to shop for chicken
and pick up the dry-cleaning,
attend social functions
that require a black dress
or maybe a small sequined hat.

I listen to your chatter
about publicists, cutbacks
in the grant system and
your New York tour.

All the while, I wonder
how you get through doctors' visits
and late night talk shows

how you rest on the August porch
listening to crickets
and leaves that rustle

how you determine
the small, sad, decisions.

Denise Coney

yellow comb
among russet pine
gentle October rain

Gloe Cormie

By the River on Opening Night

    A small dog is pulling the leash with wolverine strength. At the end of the leash, a muscular biker guy. The little bull dog, who wants to sniff each park tree, is not intimidated.

    She's purrahh muscle — this here ittybitty dawg, he says. He's dog-sitting on the prairies. I don't ask why.
Yes, he misses downhome—the country fried chicken and double Jack, misses magnolia trees, and O those southern women. He aches for their scent.

    But he's here and the day is brisk-sunny, so he's out with Flannery. The early evening opens like a stage curtain.

    Just for them.

Terrance Cox

Armstrong's Cornet

It lies in silent state —
tacky sideshow
tourist New Orleans:

draped with his white handkerchief
between its valves & bellow

baffed, its tubing
nearest mouthpiece bent

brass in several places worn
by touch & play of fingers, silver

Garish, in dissonance
hang, gilt-framed, on wall behind
1930's vintage showbills:

left, your 'Satchmo', clownish
muggin' fo' de white folks

wrong, a bow-tied 'Lou-ie' jaunts
as jewelled pun, his coronet

Not so, not on off-blue
plastic-glued-on-plywood daïs
chief lure to cheap museum

no, no, by any justice
Armstrong's cornet
ought to be enshrined

alongside Leonardo's
goose quill & oily brushes
with Galileo's stolen scope
next to Einstein's blackboard

Louis's device, no less
instrumental to our planet —

without which
it does not swing

Barbara Ruth Crupi

Last Lines: The Letter

With his letter Autumn leaves were falling;
It came too late to help him or me.
Aeons ago I'd cried out my sorrow,
Grief forming a stone deep in my heart.

Across the pages tears fell
As I turned thin paper sheets, crumpled, smudged,
Blue as his remembered eyes.
I read the dancing lines as if through pale-blue water.

Watching as memories unrolled:
Bright as colour from his artist's brush.
I was a small child, entranced, as peacock colours
Fell on canvas, surreal shapes formed.
His storminess forgotten, he hugged me close,
My loving Father.

He asks forgiveness, he left us long ago.
Can I forgive a bird for flying?

In the post another letter, he's dead I'm told:
Lying in a pauper's grave
In some solitary, back-of-beyond place.
Now there can be no reconciliation,
No grand reunion.

Yet he pleads for prayers, as if knowing death near at hand:
Asks a litany for the morning sun,
Lazy warmth on cobbled stones in an English garden.
I remember Borghese Gardens in Rome
Where, in cramped cages, leopards paced,
Dappled gold coats bright with sun.

➤

He walked silent that day,
Ignored my tight fists, fierce small face.

At the going down of the sun, he asks to remember
Huge skies of crimson stripes over Norfolk's waterways,
Amongst thin reeds emerald-headed ducks dipping . . .

At break of day, still holding his letter:
Crumpled, tear-stained from wishing back wasted, bitter years;
Say a prayer for sleep, dreamless eternal.
Redemption in that unknown distant place.

Ernest Dewhurst

Echoes of a Shot Firer

To call on him we dropped
by cage and rattled down
a slope by man-ride train.
We trudged through tunnels
ghostly-white with safety dust
then, paging the Almighty,
fumbled to the coalface-clamp
on hands and knees by rapier
beam of helmet lamps.

We did it once, as visitors.
He made a habit of the crawl.
There, cramped in two foot six
of space, he lived by firing shots
where even seven hey-ho dwarfs
would have to double up to work.

He was the human mole.

A cutter thumped its part
and in the belly of the pit
a dull thud rumbled ground.
The airspace, what there was
of it, was tight with powder
reek and dust. We choked.
On one bleak shift the mole
would fire forty shots, forty
lung-fill showers of black.
Perhaps he smelled our fear.
"If you're a worrier," he said,
"don't bother working here."

The year before a graft
of leg-pull mates had died
down where black gold
was grappled out, and quiet,
remembering them, he sighed.
"When reared to it you don't
realise the dangers here."

We blinked into the light
and longed to hug the rain.

Teacher Aunt

I saw her last in hospital,
prepared for death as all her life
she organised, was never late,
white stockings on, arms folded
on a sigh of breath, laid out
to save her nurses' time. "I'm ready
now." By morning she had died.

She died as she had lived, prepared
and punctual, a teacher minding
children like the mum she never was.
Mild as May but firm to silence boys
with left hand while the right
vamped out the morning march to hall.
In summer shepherded her urban flock
to crop some knowledge from the wild.
Slim lexicon of trees and flowers
from walks and cycle jaunts on lanes,
slipstreaming in her husband's wake.

She died as she had lived, our teacher
aunt. I see her still in slippered wool
adjusting hearing aid to coax us
into Christmas games and turns.
"You're next. What this year, Walter
de la Mare again?" Stations, pencil
paper fun. Reluctant uncles doing
forfeits underneath her non-cheat gaze.

Strictly chapel. Sermonettes for ladies
from her calligraphic notes. Girls
in movement in her rhythmics class.
She died as she had lived, prepared
and even now I hear her marching fingers
in some lofty hall. A creak of pedals
pushing home in oilskin cape, bluebells
weeping from her pannier bag. Organising
paradise, prepared and never never late.

John Dixon

Moorside

Seasons have blown away
into the mulch of years
since last I saw
the hills
like grey mould
at the sky's edge.

From sleep I've watched
the cloud herds come,
white with the August sun,
from Clwyd
where Dee mist
shrouds the months and distances.

Far sight needs days like this
of pewter skies and cold.
When last I saw so far
snow lined the eastern faces of the hills.
Memory sees it now
as if the hills, like constellations,
told us their past.
Hills I know, and stars
and days,
and not the distances between.

Fay Eagle

Lot 109: Fanscape of a Victorian Lady

Fans had marked the highlights of her life;
each one nested in a silk-lined box
until allowed to fly.

The white fan, twinkling sequins,
may have matched her first ball gown.
She would have learnt the language of the fan,
the silent code to foil her chaperone.
Held in the right hand before the face
meant follow me; twirling in the left hand
spelt leave me alone;
fanning slowly, fanning fast
the fan fluttered, flirted
at the puppeteer's command.
It is bedraggled now—a spill of wine?
Two broken sticks are badly set.

There's her wedding fan in handmade lace,
the leaf a patterning of bride and groom
and wedding bells with putti trailing flowers;
mother-of-pearl sticks gleam; in diamanté
on the guard C entwined with C:
    Clarissa—Charles.
It still looks new, used only once
and then cocooned in silk.

Pictured on her widow's fan
a woman's weeping by an urn;
black tassels give it dignity,
fashioned to her long-time mourning clothes.
It's had long usage and the silk is worn.

Gerald England

Under Macgillycuddy's Reeks

under Macgillycuddy's Reeks
rain pours relentlessly
sheep scatter as vehicle approaches
a three-way junction
two leading to where cars are banned
unless they come with four feet
smoke rises from the fire
where a tinker is encamped
yellow flowers bloom in grass
growing down the middle of roads
that climb and twist above the top
of raging waterfalls and cross
gaps between mountainsides
passing places are precarious and few
mists and clouds curl over the peaks
until we reach a remote bar
over lunch we watch the world news on TV
while the locals converse in Gaelic

Janice M. Faria

Magician

Manya's father always waited for the first
below-freezing snow-covered night
to pull the old black hose from the trap door
next to the porch and drag it across the yard
over the small brown fence into the empty lot.
Under the street light, in his red and black jacket,
puffs of breath floating in the air, he flung the hose
back and forth like a magician with his wand.
The next day before he left for the night shift
he stood by the fence, lit his pipe and watched
us come running in worn leggings and coats
from behind the coal yard, through alleys
and gangways, over the railroad tracks
to the gleaming lot, some of us balancing
on one skate, all of us learning to glide
on thin ice.

Michael Fraser

Separation

Will it always be like this between us?

a funeral of words
bundles of time caught in memory

we are mute
like two closed stones
under a woodsmoke gray sky

to love you
was to hold all of Africa
in my bare arms
to feel earth tremble and break
against my moist flesh
to taste heaven in your tongue
your cool mistral breath in summer,
now, you empty me of life

tonight, the snowshine moon
lays its fingers in your bed,
you and he are like two warm spoons
beneath white cloth,
my window's reflection
is a cage of pain,
darkness carries my words away

the distance in us
feeds the silence between these lines.

Ann Goldring

above the branch
frozen   a small bird's
small breath

juggling
the mime drops
nothing

Alistair Halden

The Other Scotland

You are the rowan tree athwart the burn,
The shifting of the shingle on the shore,
The sunlight on the far side of the valley.

You are the Sabbath peace on western isles.
You are the tolling bell on Gilmore Hill,
The beating of my heart.

You have not flinched when you have been exposed
To North Sea winds and showers of sharpened hail,
More slanted than your own historians.

You are not a wee giftie frae Rothesay,
The whisky culture of the pseudo-Gael,
All wrapped in tartan.

You are a new road through the glen,
The probing mind that seeks out ways and means,
The turbines on a thousand merchant ships.

Your dry laconic wit is self-effacing,
And people say that you are taciturn,
Prickly, and lacking in charisma.

Only your children really understand
That under your bluntness there are drops of blood.
Your dour front hides a sentimental heart.

Irene Blair Honeycutt

Stroupie in Autumn

My mountain friend keeps
hearing birds call her name.
She swears she heard them
in the woods this morning
when dawn rose behind
her cabin and this summer,
too — through her broken
windshield.
She thinks she can identify
that bird. I don't say
what I'm thinking
because it scares me and
might frighten her
although she's told me
that the only thing she's
ever feared is fire.
*I could walk through
Death's door right now,*
she said just yesterday,
cutting a path through
the air with her hands.
Lying in bed in the upstairs
room I wonder if we all
will hear some special
call.
I think of the patterns
observed in the dreams
of the dying.
Trees with one
side leafless.

Sheila Hyland

Moonlight

Your painting
Keeps me awake
All night long

Blendings of greens
In the leaves of the trees
Absorb me absolutely

I become forest
A leaf on a tree

A nightingale
Its song

Moonlight.

Ellen S. Jaffe

Night of My Conception:
Ellen's Story, Out of the Ashes, June 1944

I've always thought it began when someone died,
a child, perhaps, in the ravenous ovens.
I can see her empty shoes, discarded doll
her startled heart when gas, not water,
sprayed from the shower's nozzle, then
smoke from her last breath, yellow as the star on her sleeve
or the ghetto's last butterfly.

Quick as a wink,
in the blink of an eye,
two shakes of a lamb's tail,
mustard-coloured smoke drifts across the Atlantic,
floats like pollen from New York to California
where two people lie nervously on their makeshift bed
in a rented apartment or Quonset hut,
knowing the war is coming closer, orders
overseas could arrive any day,
any night could be their last.

June in California, the smoke turns to scent
of honeysuckle and mock-orange.
The night is warm, so quiet
you can hear icebergs melt in the Arctic.
She turns down the sheet, takes off her Snow Queen mask,
and now his hands unclench.

Some Enchanted Evening, I whisper
as I keep watch outside the window.
Birds do it, bees do it.
    Summertime,
    Someone to Watch Over Me
She opens the window wider to catch the music.
They think it's only the radio playing next door.

Beshert, someone murmurs. *It is written.*
Esther, my great-great-grandmother, appears beside me.
Suddenly petrified, I
hover
on the edge
of nothingness
of dream,
gas and smoke choking me,
scared of what lies ahead, afraid
the bed will not hold me, their arms will not hold
me.
Zisse-madela,
Esther kisses my forehead.
Sweet dreams, sweet girl.
Too surprised to hesitate
       I j u m p.

Chaco Canyon — Revisited

This pink stone, buried thousands of years,
then found again, drawing my hand like a magnet in the sand,
totem worn close to my heart,
lizard music tattooed to my skin,
gone in an instant, washed down the shower drain
      tsunami in a teacup
      Atlantis drowned in a soap-bubble
my heart constricts, the world shudders
no one has died, I tell myself,
even stones can disappear
lost pets, lost homes, lost babies
long-lost loves . . .
each parting takes us unaware.
where will the stone go on its travels?
and what will I learn from this
accident or moment of carelessness?

The week unfolds, cavern opening in the surface of things
leading to dark beyond dark,
icy ruins, hobgoblins of memory.
Turned inside out, scoured clean,
skin stripped to one thin living layer, I wash
in my own tears, salt my own wounds.
The lizard loses its tail when danger strikes,
gives up part of its body to get free, stay alive.
But where in my world is freedom, where is safety?
What happens when you make the wrong turn,
lose your tail and also your life?
The stone's lesson is in its going, teaching
me to grieve, leaving an opening
small/large enough   for love.

Hans Jongman

Coffee

After our evening meal of flounder
the water in the whistling kettle
boiling on the gas stove.
Handpoured into the linen filter
of the glazed coffeepot.
My brother and i pretended to be adults,
sipping our *koffie-verkeerd*
eating the boiling milk's slimy film,
grossing each other out.
Mother, that same evening,
would pour what coffee was left
into a glass tumbler and leave it
on the kitchen window sill.
Saved it for the husky boarder
who at 5 a.m. on his way for his
half-shift unloading river barges,
would gulp it straight down,
dead cold.

koffie-verkeerd — 1/3 coffee, 2/3 hot milk

Kristine Kaposy

haying in

thought I was rich
on two dollars and fifteen cents an hour

seven a.m. to midnight			haying in
barn shovelling watering the animals	cooking for fifteen

sat in the upstairs window			supposed to be cleaning
			hoping nobody saw
	me	see	the stallion take the mare	boarded there
for breeding
stallion's legs were too long		they had to use a platform
the three men
had to help him find his way in	kicking

Earl R. Keener

Lanterns

She called it the patriarch of goldfish,
saying the Chinese have proper respect
for carp. He'd developed an appreciation
for its fight and liked its armored look.
It was the alchemical fish, turning sludge into gold.

They talked of sex and art; of living
their lives even if it meant their undoing.
Their own words scared them.

He told her about balloons,
seen on a black branch amid ice floes:
Filled with sunlight, they seemed lanterns
of inspiration he could not attain.
Leaving, he'd almost wept.

They stood on the bridge watching
the carp sift mud, lone prospector
in a pool of cultivated trout,
then drifted toward the cemetery:

geese squabbling to the next splash of light,
asters blooming ultraviolet,
Stanislaus leaning against Goldsmith,
the graveyard a surprise party holding its breath.

Philomene Kocher

all the time now
white hairs
on the brush

Ken Kowal

after the festival

for Czeslaw Milosz

when you've kissed
all you love *good-bye,*
birthed soul, seeking
poems of a voice;
come home. we'll plant
your bones like seed
deep in soft earth.

each fall, a harvest:
poems like wheat.

this is all earth can do
for a poet. how a poet
feeds a nation's self.
how a voice cuts
the hard silence
like a knife
           the bread.

David P. Kozinski

Magic

When Chico Ruiz stole home
the pliers and hammer
no more danced on Grandfather's
off-white kitchen table.
The awl and the screwdriver
sailed off the edge, too.

Grandmother's squirrel
vaulted onto the screen
and scolded through the pantry door.

Father, from the podium,
brought down a bolt that shot
through the family's softest spot.

Offered catnip from the truck market,
the cat did nothing but roll in it;
didn't talk, open doors,
walk on his hind legs.
I laughed at my brother's
angry, feigned disappointment.

Joan Latchford

Tank

> *Arriving for a visit, I asked*
> *"Where do I go?"*

In there, is an arborite shelf
backed by a wall of smoke-tinted glass—
the embedded bars curl
decoratively.

I position myself on a stool
as in "lunch" but the counter is partitioned
as in "pawnbroker"
to afford intimacy.

We are a sorority
of girlfriends, wives, mothers
who wait, lift children nose to pane
clutching school photos.

Conversation is primal,
hard births, tubes tied after "the fourth."
I enter the circle by reassurance that a d & c
should cause only minimal bleeding.

Then—all swivel, to pick up the handsets
as their menfolk swim into view—
uniformed goldfish
in an aquarium.

John B. Lee

The Chair of Angels

for Brother Paul Quenon

The Shakers
made their brooms
from cornstraw
stalwart enough to sweep
the stars away
and yet
the dew-wet webs
that draped the fences
like beaded purse skeins
stayed their strength
small spiders spun
between white boards
an iron beauty there
to catch the light
that sleepers cannot see
though saved for them
by tiny flaws of mayfly fate
in a crush of ragged wings.

And these Shakers made such chairs
so strong and briefly perfect
that the angels
might alight
upon them, weightless
as the hollow bones of birds.

One time, entire yards
of Seraphim came down
to walk the lawns and watch
while looking out the windows
from their work
the craftsmen
spokeshaved to an awe
so knurled it fit the dove
like buttermelt
and all the heavens
were a sheet of light . . .
"come in," they said
"sit down"
and every chair
went brilliant in their hands
and welcome
was a simple breath of wings.

Red Barns

Last century
there was blood in the paint
on the boards of these barns.
Ontario, I have seen
the bleeding of a slaughtered sky
in the western hemorrhage
at the death of the day
in the morbid menses
of a moon-timed afternoon
and thought of beauty dying
where it rubs the world away
in that the last of light
while somewhere else along the waking curve
young hours
warm the latches
on a dreaming door
and though a distant window sulks with rain
and pond mist
drifts like something burning slow
among the singing fogs
the blackbird's flashing wing
wags off the weed in flame
and dove flutes
mourn their flight
ah, moralizing angels, pass above these mortal barns
they bear the proof of lambs
gone silent on our knives
they have the memory of hog's lament
the sorrowing away
of market sows
the knackered beast
who proves his barrow's heart
is emptied as a well-squeezed rag

and all the sweeter crimson drums
have dripped dark zeros full to the flux
that's quivered to final stillness in the ox
as thirsty cedar waits
to the very mow-boards
of these family farms
we've ghosts enough
to last us into unborn dust
make ashy berms from all romance
the fertile strangers yet to meet
and couple and decline
and this an awful art
behold the pigment of each generation's fate
red barns have much to expiate.

Walking Along Lake Erie

Some Sundays when my cousins were home
Uncle John would take us
in the truck
down dirt roads
in a trail of amber dust
that floated up and out
like junk-hole smoke let crawl
across the high flat fields
left to scrub thorn
and nettles fallowed by brambles
clarifying to the green crop-wreck of weeds
where poor farmers lived
in clinker-built clapboards time-chafed
on the cliffs above Clearville
and Palmira
and we would walk
where the grass and vines
were espaliered against the bluffs
by the prevailing rain-wasped
breath of God
where the lake had lost its blue
becoming eluant as wash water
and we stepped to where we saw
the scrap of sun-bleached water dark
driftwood like old-boned men
lying hip and thigh
in the shallow surf
some of it rocking a little
as if locked in the swell and go
of remembered love.

And we gathered fish floats
made into grey-green telescopes to watch
the turn of gulls
we collected the best-pearled shells
to catch the sun glint
and think of something
concerning the inside of ourselves
we came upon and crossed
the muddy privilege of each chill stream
threading its meaning
in a larger thought and being gone
we looked up gullies
and ravines
where spools of fence wire
fell in curled perimeters of measured rust
and old half-chassised automobiles
forgot themselves and found
ferruginous purpose returning to the earth
in slow mustard-coloured rills.

And we ran and ran
until we stopped, breathing hard
our hearts beating like storm-blind birds
under where the root-nests clung
and the doomed trees leaned
and it was only several hours
once or twice a year
we went sandpipering
to where the autumn ended
and the bent branches
revealed another season

➤

where the thick-hipped cliff
came over-close
and the lake refused us
unwanted as we were in the indolent erosions
of some larger work.

Paying Attention
for Mike Wilson

We look down from the hill
and see where the small
and seemingly inconsequential swale
winters below us
and know that it is one of the last precious places
and all along the hogback
we are silent
all down the snow-loud slope
we are wordless
in the slowing of spirit
beneath the beauteous wing span
of God's best creature
riding the waves of heat
above the sun-brilliant meadow
a lone golden eagle
displays its white underwing
working the love of being alive
in the heights
and then
in this landscape
of rough-bark cherry
and larch   and the last leaf rattle of low weeds
we come upon the green hallucination
of balsam, a small stand
of colour, and the cedar hush
blind beyond the edges
and know that we are wrong
to ever call the thick dark and deep interior
shadow or shade

➤

it is rather
an artful absence of light
as it is within pure and wordless thought
where we learn the awe
of watching wild turkeys walk
like black scraps in the far valley
and deer grazing the ripe nub of pine
under the bald eagle's flush
and the vulgar profanity of crows.

"Crows love to swear,"
my companion says.
"Hear how they curse that fellow's coming.
See there, they've set guards above the deer blow
sentinels surrounding
the racket we make breaking trail."
My friend bends down
to show me the fragile downy fronds of ice rim
where the deer track
punched a pre-dawn path
and I see how cold and sunless walking
leaves evidence of its hour
how we might read the thorns
for blood spray
how on the trail of ghosts we seem
and yet in the deep available knowing of nature
it longs to reveal itself and be revered
we simply speak of eagles
and they arrive hovering
above where God is making windows
on the lake.

And I apprehend the truth of wishing
something in the poet-lonely
universe, I realize
the purpose of our being
glimpse it in how this single
solitary man
might save us all
by holding out his hand palm up and open
wherein a swamp secret sits
a single salamander, rare
small, delicate as elderberry pluck.

Anne Lewis-Smith

Little Haven at Low Tide

Walking the beach in wellingtons
the roaring sea, caged by an ebbing tide,
stretches white claws across the sand.

Seven metres point three
at sixteen hundred hours.
Two hours before the turn.

Finger-nail shells lie unbroken
necklacing the wet strand.
Strange that such fierce breakers
can leave fragility
uncrushed, and yet
hurl pebbles in their curve.

How can these savage waves
with rollers racing in
be ebbing out?

In eight hours time, this space,
this air I breathe,
will all be drowning sea.

Shore running foam
quick tongues at me
to lick my boots.
I do not trust those lists
of water high and low,
fearing all currents' deadly drag.

Reaching the high-tide litter line
of plastic bottles, orange ropes
I am beyond that creature's reach.

I shall be drinking tea
behind my sandbagged door
when that unceasing beast
explodes with rage against the cliff,
spits spume against my window-panes,
at four o'clock.

Dun Aonghasa, Aran

Here is the hub
of my mind's
quiet turning,
the greased ease
of thinking.

Behind me
great grey stones
placed each on each
rise in a high
protective curve,
their ends cut short
by space—
a space
where land should be.

There, at the edge,
winds slice sharp
and seabirds rocket up
eighty empty metres
from cold uneasy sea.

I am water,
wind, rock and gull,
have slammed cliffs,
sent spray flying,
caught and blown
fine salty drops high,
high to my great
horseshoe of stones —

> I have always
> been here

Noah Leznoff

pushing in the grocery line

and it's all fine, a tight thursday, till the sudden
opening of a new register. that, and our standing
elbow-to-elbow from the free lane—me and the black-
draped crow, end-of-week hag whose brain's
   some feral abacus clicking:
the number of carts in each line
the number of items per basket
the relative efficiency of sandy or k.c.
or jean. *can I help the next in line, please?*
yeah, and i'm out first with a head-fake
or maybe she is; anyway, it's started: our steps
quicken like those skittering xylophonic
birds', sandpipers'; open-coated, carts
rattling, a bit of the hip as we log-jam
kitty-corner at the wafer and tabloid rack.
   and here's adept thickness! her jaw
flummery but fierce, eyes stone
blank to my gritted nods and smiles,
begging sardonic pardon, inching basket
of steel (but she's nudging too! staring clear through
me, staring through and leaning hard
so that but for the force of her in my wrists
and forearms i know what it means
to be invisible. do you laugh or swat her,
take her by the throat or in your arms? i'm seeing
turn-of-the-century furrows, ox cart tracks thick
in the mud, potatoes, a sandy-haired farm boy crazy
with wonder for the strength of her kiss
—that boy running home, swinging his arms
wide at the scend of an open blue hill
   trying to fly because of her. have i kissed
the crone, her tongue like moss?
Babi-Yaga!! here's yelling, confusion, people:
and outside a rush-hour horn blast
and the sudden-cold darkness coming fast

Robert Lima

After an Anonymous Eighth-Century Gaelic Poet

That long cold day in Great Moor
foreshadowed devastating nights
with rain, no trifle, lashing through
the ancient wood that sheltered life,
the clean wind howling a great roar.

The gusts had broken his resolve,
had crushed the poet's spirit with
their great, relentless icy thrusts,
had drowned him in his human plight.
He suffered endlessly in time!

To voice his sad condition to the King,
(upon the distant star-bright throne),
like Job before his deity, who lacked
a sense of human suffering or need,
he wrote the pain in "Wind" and "Storm."

The poems shout of wind consuming life
like twigs beset by raging crimson fire
ordained by Heaven for a purpose that
the poet's reason cannot quite surmise.
There was no course but deep despair.

His grief took form in plaintive words
that still describe our meager state
(a hopeless fear yet shakes the mien
when Nature's elemental powers rear).
There is no respite from the cruel wind.

Norma West Linder

Sonnet for Martha

You took my writing classes years ago
—your husband brought you in a wheelchair.
If you were scared, you didn't let it show.
You were so young; it seemed so damned unfair.
Later, throughout the years, our paths would cross
at concerts, in the mall, or on the street;
we'd talk of books you'd read, of Sinclair Ross
and once of your divorce. Each time we'd meet
I'd find you failing, hard to understand
and would, in passing, merely touch your hand.

Your words appeared in newsprint at the end:
We can live many lives if we can read.
You could rely on books. Martha, Godspeed.
I wasn't brave enough to be your friend.

Mikal Lofgren

Winter Touching the Bones

Snowlight
fills the rooms.
Cold polishes the senses,
radiates off the windows,
falls to the floor.

The brittle night
whittles away warmth,
pares flesh from bone
in a shiver.

The pale glow
kisses the marrow,
freezes its sweetness,
leaves it
a suet for winter birds
when bones are frozen away.

Robin Lovell

nesting birds scurry
glean winter debris
from the graves

cemetery path
buried by leaves
a shoe among them

Neil mac Neil

Sow the Good Seed

You said I cannot come to the poem
as you do to the field.
That I merely sow, grow, reap

from the word, from its seeds
of mysteries and sacrifices
harvested for centuries.

There, you burn the forest back
in Peten, in tropical Tikal.
But the world appears smokeless here.

From here with no pyramids
to sight movements of stars,
with no Mayan or Toltec Teocallis
to measure the summer, the winter solstice

we act unlike priests at the time
of maximum rainfall
or at the end cycle of seasons.

I do not know how or when
to dress for the binding ritual,
the one that holds the earth

in orbit through sun and rain
of stars, the rise and fall of life
on the river flood plain.

There moonlight hammers home
on limestone, on sandstone,
drawing shadows of plumed serpents

as long word seeds asleep in Yucatan.
Here, the still undeciphered stones
of Callanish, or the ring in Orkney

seem a far cry from Guatemala,
the politically incorrect calculations
of astronomy, cosmic husbandry,

worship, solar economics.
We both plant vowels and consonants
La Naya. Naranjo. Quezaltenago.

Sow the good seed.
Words beyond the river basin.

Giovanni Malito

Sarnia, Ontario, 1981

I was just like you,
a man too (qualified
the month before)
sitting there next to you
in that greasy spoon
fuelling up for the tomorrow
and the refinery,
saying nothing except
in whispers to my food,
the blue plate special —
chops, mashed potatoes
and limp green beans —
and I was learning fast
watching you, how to
push back the plate,
swivel on my stool,
throw down some coins
and get out, fast.

Joy Hewitt Mann

It is the moon

that fits like a white circle on
black paper; or a pupil-
less eye in a dark face.
It is the magnet of a moon
on a dark fridge; a round
hole in a black curtain
that hides us from eternity.

That night it was only a moon, a
cold planet we learned about in school
and the sky was a mother's voice
calling us home.

We walked linked through the corn
free arms swinging against the shushing leaves
stroking the silken tassels with tingling palms
fingers conscious of being, of
needing something concrete to touch.

Our emotions collided in those
clenched hands; they
copulated with the rhythm of our
walking. We
were as innocent as young whores
in our longing for something beyond the corn,
the sky,

the moon.

Why I should think of you,
a child, now that I have
children of my own,
I do not know. It is
a perversion more stimulating
that a Chinese egg, round
and white as a full moon pushed
deep into my inner sky. Why

should I think of you, staring
from my bedroom window, stroking
silken tassel with tingling palm
hearing the shush of my own blood

wondering if it is
the moon?

What Nobody Knows About Spring at the Seniors' Home

Nobody knows that it is not the effort
of designing their summer garden
holds Winifred and Maggie's minds
in abeyance. They sit silent
as the sun slides by the windows of the enclosed porch
over their glyphic faces, over
the brims of weeding hats bought at the latest church
bazaar. It is not
that their flesh is asleep to the solar caress
or indifferent — as they are to death
and other trivialities — it
is the men who are now as detached from them
as the white house-fronts across the street;
the shirtless men working on the snow-worn roofs
watched from under eyelids
that rise like the flaps of dewed tents,
and lagging chins that tighten, lift
to point to young, muscled backs and dark hair that moves
in the breeze.
The women's minds are inundated with sun
and air
and dreams of how their bodies
were once
forever.

Nobody knows they once were loved
by Joseph sagging beside them;
a scholar of green things, replying with his shaky hands
to the open speech of summer, once so sure
that what he wrote in the ground would turn away death.
He silently stares, distrusts
the garden that waits for him to go, for it, he knows,
will always be here. All
growing things now hold his tongue hostage and his heart
feels the earth will never forgive him for his pride
but pull him as surely as he once pulled weeds
with hands as gnarled and browned now as dead roots.

Nobody would guess that Winifred, Maggie and Joseph
meet each Wednesday for strip poker, each
with their favorite wild-card game:
Winifred and Maggie know that Jacks are wild and
Kings too often abdicate; Joe
hopes his heart will hold, his spade stay true.

Nobody knows
they have been hoarding pills since fall;
slipping an extra ace
up their sleeves.

John E. Marks

Working Girl

A pleasure-seeker, petulant, pruned hard,
Stepping out, a girl of fifty, gin-drinker,
Rouged and randy, she bandies words.
Hair styled, clothes perfumed, no excesses
Of taste. Nothing smeared or wrinkled here.
A tinkle of bangles as she lifts her drink.
Dressed up, for the night, tight and squirmy.
She looks around. She smiles as she sees
The man's face. He pulsates. No hotel room service
This. No head-shrieking beast. But a hardened
Release. This evening he's the last in a line.
She knows there'll be another. There's time.

Ben Murray

First Night

early 60's Illinois —

a couple of poverty-line librarians
de-porch, retreat from renegade
Windy City winds, his pipe left smoldering
on peeling bird-do railing
her cat's-eye glasses perched on wicker
left to watch birds swallowing the dusk

inside, the house creaks, groans,
sighs, housetalk echoing their walk
through shivering rooms
their four feet meeting
in the upstairs bedroom with prints of
Mondrian and Macke for windows

the bed beckons in the save-gas lose-heat
chill, pj-ed bodies clutch and de-shiver
skin-shy flesh welcoming the no-light of night —
within minutes flannel becomes sweat
made wearable, unwearable

and in half an hour or so
a mom and dad are born

and as I journey from one to the other
I wonder at this leap of faith
this pantomime we three enact

the animal cries of my parents
caged and released
behind these windowless walls

Sue Nevill

Mother/daughter/portrait

You do not recognize yourself.
Jealously, you ask who that woman is
cheek to cheek with me, our skins scored
in identical lines, our eyes equally rounded
and ready to smile. Identified,
you laugh and laugh, as I
sink into silence.
Mirrors are clouded to you now,
no give and take from glass to mind.
Are you lost? Are you going?
Without a firm reflected outline,
how do you find yourself these days
in the long unmarked hours?
Bit by bit, you are pared away —
a brain cell, a whisper of flesh,
a flick of concentration —
until I cannot recognize myself
in you. Except for the eyes,
the laughter.

azimuths

1

you are drawn
to things that can carry you away
small boats   music
anything resembling
a train

in art you prefer
the faintly pencilled
horizon   your own drawings
have no frames

2

words do not travel well
they lose their edge
words are no longer
a weight you can carry gladly

look
at the power of one charcoal line
extending margins

Renee Norman

My Father, Driving

I am sitting in the back seat
of the white Pontiac
on the way back from the hospital
(no children allowed)
but my father visited Uncle Mel
dying of cancer
and I only understand the sadness
in the car like an extra passenger:
we're giving a ride to Grief

I hear my father's words
we hang onto life no matter what
the way I am gripping
the upholstery of the front seat
in the days with no seatbelts
emotions flying all over the interior

it's pitch black
a Calgary morning in congested traffic
but at least the snow's abated
and the seatbelts are state of the art
my sister is driving my father to the hospital
there they insert a needle
through his shoulder to the tip of his liver
passing through a lung
I'm not in the car
not even in the city
and for weeks I have been talking to my father
through my mother
inserting care and concern in the phone lines
passing by the heart

➤

when I finally speak to my father
I tell him I love him
pray for the best
listen to the dignity and courage
of words profound with 82 years of driving:
what will be, will be

someone comments:
when you're that age every day is a gift
I think the gift is a man in a white Pontiac
my father, driving
and I'm in the back seat again
holding on
holding on

H.F. Noyes

        season's end —
        all the autumn color
        in one leaf

full moon rising
the far-flung seines
catch only stars

                up bright and early
                arranging flowers
                to look unarranged

Anne-Marie Oomen

Ode to Dirt in an Old Farmer's Lungs

To tell it simply as it happened,
just after the surgery on his colon
took out two tumors, the one they
knew about, the other a mushroomed surprise,
and how they found the blockage in his lungs,
down at the bottom they said, and how
they also said it might be simple to fix,
not even another surgery, but instead,
an apparatus with a mist of expectorant,
and that it began to clear after only three days—
is to go at it all wrong.

What granules from dry clay—
what soiled molecules rising from the drought
he plowed through in eighty-two—
what constellations of mud dripping
into his panting mouth—
what dark clots spit from furrows,
kicked into his face from the wheels
of a muck-covered Allis Chalmers—
what manic wind across a two-forty plot
where he spread manure for fifty years—
what building of loam—leaning into it, tasting it,
breathing it into his cells—earthen alveoli
where emptiness had been—what
chemistry of dust!

When the mucus spilled up,
they tested it, said it was just dirt.
He asked if there was enough to grow
anything, if they could check the PH.
(A small joke in light of all the tests.)
After that he stared out the hospital window
at a flat roof that would grow nothing;
folded the pillars of his arms, looking
like Samson after they cut his hair,
like a man from whom something
had been taken.

Kathy Pearce-Lewis

Aubade

Now in the morning I miss you.
Wrapped in the dawn's cold
I remember the long loaf
of your body warm against me
the first movement toward me
and the day's love rising.

Linda Vigen Phillips

Dress Rehearsal

Before departing, I gathered bread
and wine, and other staples
organized them into meaning
to be consumed by my family.

I made all beds
(not neglecting cat and bird)
closed all doors
left only a small pile
of laundry.

The sun touches my right cheek;
driving south, Pachelbel's canon lifts
tires above the earth
and we sail across sandhills
like cows over moons.

Turning west now, all gold on blue
pines submit in unison
to a kite-less March wind
pointing the way into dazzling bright.

A perfect moment
suspends in mid-air,
riding breathless on the crest
of a baroque melody.
If you looked back now
you would see a well-spring of life
cascading, crystal clear
down the highway.

My hands stretch
to the light, brilliant
and silent
calling my bones.

Peggy Poole

Fête de la Musique, Geneva

In the square (meeting place
in pre-Roman times, rendez-vous
for today's students), watched
by admiring mothers, fathers drinking beer,
three-year-olds weaving in and out of tables,
young voices sing old spirituals
(Nobody knows the trouble I've seen)
lifting that load of suffering
to float in June's evening light.

Tall apartments lean towards each other
to savour the sound. Shoppers
and visitors from Korea, Ghana
Iran and Mexico stop,
as chattering sparrows stop,
to catch and store the moment
secure against the future.

Al Purdy

House Guest

> *for Milton Acorn*

For two months we quarrelled over socialism   poetry
                              how to boil water
doing the dishes   carpentry   Russian steel production figures
                         and whether
you could believe them and whether Toronto Leafs would take it all
that year and maybe hockey was rather like a good jazz combo
never knowing what came next
Listening
how the new house built with salvaged old lumber
bent a little in the wind and dreamt of the trees it came from
the time it was travelling thru
and the world of snow moving all night in its blowing sleep
while we discussed ultimate responsibility for a pile of dirty dishes
Jews in the Negev   the Bible as mythic literature   Peking Man
and in early morning looking outside to see the pink shapes of wind
printed on snow and a red sun tumbling upward almost touching
                         the house
and fretwork tracks of rabbits outside where the window light had lain
last night an audience
watching in wonderment the odd human argument
that uses words instead of teeth
and got bored and went away

Of course there was wild grape wine and a stove full of Douglas fir
(railway salvage) and lake ice cracking its knuckles
                                      in hard Ontario weather
and working with saw and hammer at the house
                                      all winter afternoon
disagreeing about how to pound nails
arguing vehemently over how to make good coffee
    Marcus Aurelius   Spartacus   Plato and François Villon

And it used to frustrate him terribly
that even when I was wrong he couldn't prove it
and when I agreed with him he was always suspicious
and thought he must be wrong because I said he was right
Every night the house shook from his snoring
a great motor driving us on into daylight
and the vibration was terrible
Every morning I'd get up and say "Look at the nails—
you snored them out half an inch in the night—"
He'd believe me at first and look and get mad and glare
and stare angrily out the window while I watched
                                    10 minutes of irritation
drain from his eyes onto fields and farms and miles and miles
                                      of snow

We quarrelled over how dour I was in early morning
and how cheerful he was for counterpoint
and I argued that a million years of evolution
from snarling apeman have to be traversed before noon
and the desirability of murder in a case like his
and whether the Etruscans were really Semites
the Celtic invasion of Britain   European languages   Roman law
we argued about white being white (prove it dammit) & cockroaches
bedbugs in Montreal   separatism   Nietzsche   Iroquois
                              horsebreakers on the prairie
death of the individual and the ultimate destiny of man
and one night we quarrelled over how to cook eggs
In the morning driving to town we hardly spoke
and water poured downhill outside all day for it was spring
when we were gone with frogs mentioning lyrically
Russian steel production figures on Roblin Lake which were almost nil
I left him hitch hiking on #2 Highway to Montreal
and I guess I was wrong about those eggs

Lynn Veach Sadler

As Silent as Mimes

In Buenos Aires' San Telmo antique market,
an old dancer has taken her accustomed place
on the street of entry amid mimes
and jewelry hawkers.
She is as silent as the mimes,
only fanning forth a pirouetting hand,
palm upward, to invite your inspection
of her wares.
A rigged clothesline with costumery
on rusting hangers.
On the ground at her feet
a cloth of faded blue velvet
cradling pictures in cracking frames
of her dancing
the tango with different partners,
every one younger than the one before.
A young boy, perhaps her grandson,
stands to the side, bored, shuffling cards.
An early-model Polaroid
waits on the sidewalk at his side.
If you choose to have your picture made,
you choose, too, your costume: cape,
hat, once-white shirt with ruffled front.
The boy slicks your hair back
at his grandmother's direction.
She teaches you the tango pose.
You must practice with her
until you can carry it off
to her satisfaction.
She will not have her picture
made with a female,
though she deigns to dress her
in a tango gown and shoes,

looking disdainfully at the size of her feet.
What the old woman really wants from you
is payment to watch her dance the tango.
The boy plays the music on a wind-up
record player accommodating 78's.
When the music starts,
people crowd around, point and whisper
until the dancer starts her flight.
They go as silent as the mimes
to watch the feat before them.
In the city where Eva Peron is buried,
in the city of the
Mothers of the Disappeared,
the old dancer of the tango
resurrects a fallen world.

Joanna Catherine Scott

What Time Does

'My impotence,' you say, apologetically,
as though this condition you have come to
is some stray dog slunk through your door
that will not be shooed off. In despair,
you've learned to love it, let it follow you around.
Down the street it comes, padding along
behind you on importuning feet, scrambling
into bed with you, crowding out the lovers
you would take if this creature were not
right there, barking its foolish head off,
refusing to be pushed away, or kicked away,
or locked out in the hall. Night by night you lie
dreaming of the angel who will come, one day,
soft-voiced and smiling, offering poisoned bait.

Jeff Seffinga

Spring's First Crop

Every spring, the first crop from the field
sloping toward the snow-melt creek
was always stone.
Heaved to the surface by winter's deep frost,
any rock bigger than a fist
had to be pulled from the clutching earth
before plowing could begin.

Over land too soft for tractors
old Herman, the big-footed, gentle horse,
dragged the stoneboat in sure straight lines
while we, in mud-clotted boots,
marked and loosened stones, small boulders,
waited until the stoneboat's pass
to roll or tuck them onto its low platform.

Spades and pry bars clanked on granite;
scrape of the stoneboat, clink
of Herman's traces against the whippletree,
blended with the grunts and heaves
as straining arms and backs rolled rocks
onto the thick plank sledge.
Each load was delivered to the field's perimeter.

McCann, the neighbor to the north,
said, Dump them, pile them any way. Cattle
won't cross, they're too afraid they'll break
their legs without solid footing.
But no, we had to build a solid wall
of the gathered stones, largest boulders on the bottom
and three feet wide at least, high as our waist,
the small stones filling chinks and cracks
sometimes tamped in place with a blacksmith's hammer.

➤

One wide low stone wall, the result
of years of springtime effort, enhanced
the symmetry of cleared field,
the long intact lines of plowed furrows,
the even rows of corn growing to harvest.
Harvest would be easier, without curses
of broken machine parts, with the pride
of unbroken effort, a sense of work well done.
As fertile and smooth as a mother's bosom
the field glowed with our quiet satisfaction.

Shirley A. Serviss

Sowing words

It is not what I remember
my father saying, but the things
unsaid: his tears
in the car on the way into town
after fighting with my sister

It is not his letters, but his
lack of letters: his name
laboriously inscribed on the
down payment for my first house
—the cheque sewn into the lining
of his best suit for the flight
to Kelowna

It is his silence, his loss
of words: the night I told him
I was leaving my husband—
my husband was leaving me

It is those last days where only
an eyelid fluttered, a breath
faltered. It is to fill the pauses,
the barren page, the empty
traces, the fallow field:
I write about my father

K.V. Skene

In Like a Lion

Quick terrible movements,
silent claws,
      eyes

that strip sky to wounded bird,
      earth to trembling mouse,
        night to hunger. God/Lover

with you I am only body, breath
prey. I am
the open veldt burnt

into your brain. Heart/Soul
of lion, unringed by hope,
      untamed by a history

not your own. Your death
tongues my thin skin, muscle, bone,
nothing is born

by chance. I never knew
my own darkness, my own hunger
to kill.

Tammara Or Slilat

Atonement Day

The soothing gong of silence
hangs above the Jordan valley
as a hawk caught in mid-air.
It's the Day of Atonement today,
even the hawk knows it, and
the deer, they dare
cross the empty roads.

Marvin Smith

Visiting Ray Chapman's Grave

You were beaned, Ray, high and fast,
The seamed missile hurled hard cutting
Half the crisp diagonal of a summer square,
Splitting the ruled emerald geometry of life.

And now we visit you through tall gates,
Visit your story at a plain granite block
Surrounded by ostentatious angels, Ray,
By the weeping marble maidens you'll never see.

You'd think they'd rule your plot with a limed line,
Leave a base pad for your pillow; but keepers
Of this field know only oak and dogwood,
Low hills and the game of graceful curves.

A brown bag rests on your headstone, Ray.
No forget-me-nots nor plastic lilies
Mark your remembrance. Just an old Indians' pin,
A can of beer and a plug of Union Square.

Raymond Souster

Love Birds

Doesn't take very much to startle me
these days: but that sudden crashing
against our back picture window
early this afternoon, had me spinning around
to see what was happening now.

And it's love that's happening
as twin birds thrust away
at their own speed of sound,
and going with a whirl of joy
in their twisting flight
our *Snowbirds* might envy:

their "knock-knock, who's there?"
brief tattoo against our window,
enough to push me wildly
out the door into spring.

While the Smog Burns Off

Two extra morning sounds
thrown in at no extra charge:

one mild-mannered diesel train,
one jet-liner's throat-clearing roar.

And trying to get into the act,
an ambulance bearing down
on the nearest intersection,
with its hell-for-leather,
death-is-serious scream.

The Bird Who Somehow Could Not Fly

As I walked by the hedge at the corner,
from out of its close-cropped leafy centre
a sparrow fluttered weakly up, brushed me on the wrist,
then scurried out of sight again,
but this time strictly on the ground.

Was it frightened at my approach?
Could it have been a plea for help?
No way to tell, of course;
but still I've been blessedly touched
by another living creature
before my day is even one hour old.

Margaret Speak

Set to Last

Boneweary he sat, the paper a tent across
his stomach, hand collaring his working boots
set ready for cobbling beside a piece of hide
a neat rectangle the colour of weak tea
curled slightly, the leather shop clung to its curve.

Kate saw him choose this piece, discard others
too thin or shiny, dealing them patiently
on the wooden counter, Tom stacking them back,
their conversations economical as poker players.
Tom played close, made Dad sort the pack.

He slid out deftly a piece from under,
with a sly grin to be matched by Dad's,
scooped tingles and sprigs inside paper twists
gave those to her with humbugs magicked from his sleeve
the mint taste oozed into the brown smell of the shop.

With a gentle hiss of breath like iron steam
he sighed, folded his paper precisely, began,
wrapping his apron round, front-tied the strings.
Like a solemn apprentice she copied and watched:
they could hear the bubbles of gas in the coals.

His tongue mimed the boots' curled up
in concentration, his brow textured as leather.
He eased a pencil stub around the sole, cut it
with a razor blade. Kate lifted his polished boot
foot creased, walked it on her hand.

Dad levered the old sole, brittle and thin
tore free the tonsure of leather
with its picket of nails, set the boot upon the last.
His grip locked the hammer, brought it down
sharp, accurate, tacking the sole.

Brownball wax tucked under the tip of the iron;
he nodded and she set it to heat, rocker-shaped
on the grate, while he pared the leather edge
and she crayoned wax around its curve.
He ironed it smooth and the brown smell steamed.

Dad fingered tobacco in his pipe;
Kate fetched brushes, Kiwi tin, the velvet pad
and smeared polish, he brushed the shine
but she buffed them with a velvet heart, saw his smile
reflected as he leaned them against the fender.

Elizabeth St Jacques

Points of Light

sunrise . . .
the pond slowly fills
with lotus blooms

after the storm
my window filled —
double rainbow

stop light
old nun stoops to gently lift
the limp butterfly

points of light
on the sunset beach —
an Orca's eyes

moonless night
among forest ferns
glowworms

prairie darkness
our motorcycle following
the North star

cold moon
the watchful wolf
glistening with frost

Christmas morn
in his small cupped hands
a gift of sparkling snow

Sandra Staas

Turning the Coals

Father's purple hands reach forward.
Palms misshapen maps flick
pages of faded photographs
of Africa, natives, the jungle,
where a hot sun sears the paper
and ashes scatter to earth.
Smoke trickles over the earth,
creeps messages into dark crevices,
carves new life from dried petals.
Father of the soil
from where flowers become God
and death a mere turn of the page.
Gone before I knew you.
Gone before I feared you.
Left me to become you.
Left me to venture alone along
bloodstained paths where parched
earth crumbles at each step.
Where conquerors shell and the fallen weep.
Words crackle in the flames,
cinders char his bones.

Jean Stanbury

Tribute

*The Commando Memorial
Spean Bridge*

They trained
deep in Lochaber hills,
forded icy lochs
scaled the unscalable
burrowed deep in peat
lay low from live bullets.

Cast stern in bronze
three commandos stand,
firm, rooted in rock,
upstaging
grim mountain ranges

reminder:
of lives lost at Dieppe,
on Normandy beaches,
of death
among the heather.

Valerie Stetson

Wedding Story Love

wedding story love
is stoned with content
it thrives in small
Mennonite communities
where it cannot dance
and ravishes the
Alberta winter

a chinook in shirtsleeves
it gallops down basement steps
toward the noise
which becomes a cat
everything comes easily, even trouble
is carved into a string of hearts

undressed before
an uncertain future
wedding vow love
worships with its body
uncrumples its fist
repeating words
that have come before
with faith

Sheila Stewart

Ladybones

Why do I think of your collarbone, what could be made of it? A flute, a whistle, smooth like bone-handled knives, the good set tucked away in a felt bag, the everyday ones growing yellow. I want to know its exact shape. Want to rub it smooth, bone gone to ashes, ashes far away, nothing in my hand, the bones the Swazi healers threw to tell us our future, what to do, whom to appease, the bones of ancestors rising up to cast our lot, a bone falling from a tree.

I think of you dry as a bone. Are you thirsty, do I pick out the bones of the story?

And your son's bones? Bones with osteomyelitis, bones falling, bones that broke, that left him with a brace on his leg, so you said, *keep it out of sight for the photo.*

Why do I want you *Skinny Malink Malone, Skinny Bones?* You, the slim, delicate one, your father said, *every farm should be able to support one lady*, your lady bones. My wishbone.

Hipbones letting forth daughters, my bones open and loose, how I shake them, spine elongated, a hundred bony bones in this hand moving.

Andrew Stickland

A Midsummer-Night's Lament

Beneath the hot, hot weight of night
I can hear the soft and midnight sea
Across the empty beach. Like brief applause
The slow percussion of waves and of waves…

And somewhere close, between the molten dark
And the moonlit walls, cicadas gather
To squeeze their plain-song, line by line,
From the heavy, breathless cloth of the air.

Closer still, the hum-hum-hum of electric blades
Above my head carves the night's threnody
To slabs of monotone, to a funereal bass
Repeating and repeating and repeating.

And here, beneath it all, my own harsh melody
Is the rustle of a single, restless sheet
Playing over the damp heat of my skin,
And a long sigh, lost, like a prayer ignored.

Lynn Tait

Mother and Son

I remember when he held my hand,
insisted on it,
though no longer a baby
or even a toddler.

Regret the times
I insisted he walk
unfettered by my fingers,

now that I miss those cheeks
that once fit into the palm of my small hand,
fail to see why I wished his high-pitched voice
would break into deepening tones.

Was I preparing myself
for the cut ties,
the growth that leans away…

Am I nothing more than a loose string
unraveling at the slightest tug,
a wayward strand of hair
pushed back in annoyance
or without much thought?

I'm tempted to shake him back into my life
like a furious snow scene trapped in glass.
At the same time, want to close my eyes,
plug my ears, wish for ignorance,

and ground him when flashes of myself —
ripples in the gene pool — wash over me
in a cold shudder like an October lake;
afraid history will repeat itself…

afraid he will swim in a sea of delusions
reaching shore too late,
waterlogged with regret
and blaming me
for the lateness of the hour.

Adèle Kearns Thomas

Runaway

Truant from cloister
within terraced shale,

nomadic spring
    is purified,
struggles
through meshwork
    of root & pebble

drooling
    over cutting edge rock
swatched
    in yellow-green
        lichens,

nearly earth-sucked
    by humus
unfazed loner
    wriggles
around broomstick pine,

sly as slinking cat
    in lean-to shadows,

slips into foolproof stream
    groined
        sand-banked
designed for permanence,

Dreams
of a breathing sea
that will make room for it.

Carolyn Thomas

gathering creek stones
in the tail of my sweatshirt
last days of autumn

lake water
moves
with no sound;
even the crows are silent
this cold grey evening

Stephen Threlkeld

Good-morning

Five-grain granola cereal
The Israelis killed a terrorist
His wife and his small son
And the milk is on the turn
At the end of the garden
The cat stalks a sparrow
Or is it a cat stalks the sparrow
The potted blue hyacinths
Fill the room with
Incense-like perfume
But they no longer stand erect
The early sun cuts across the lawn
And enters the room
A woman's hair becomes a halo
There is blood in the snow
Israel is eight hours away
And there are snow-drops in the garden
Will they survive
If the temperature drops to minus five
They say the double star Sirius A
Is eight light-years away
Fifty trillion miles away
The sweet delicious luxury
Of sweet China tea
The smell of bacon frying
The crispy bits are best
Is the sparrow still alive
Is there still time for tea
'Stands the clock at ten to three'
Did they die instantly
The astronomers say
SS 433 is fifteen thousand
Light-years away.

Mildred Tremblay

Codeine and Roses

for Mae Hill Brown

We split a gingerale
the old poet and I.
Here's to you, friend.
Our conversation unfolds,
old fabric, stroked
and ironed out with words.

We talk about husbands—she recalls
the day of her wedding.
September, nineteen thirty-two.
The winds of the Great Depression
whistled through everyone's coat.

For the party, her mother
somehow managed a miracle:
Chicken à la king, elegantly
served in shells for her daughter.
All the neighbours were invited.

She remembers her father. Anxious
and clumsy with love, he put his foot
through her veil, ripped the muslin.

Sixty-five years have gone by.
Her mother, her father with his foot,
the long-ago neighbours
are all bones in the graveyard.

She sighs. All week she has struggled
with pain. At night it is *exquisite*,
she says. Codeine doesn't touch it.
But, she confides, just before dawn
the petals of that rose
on the table were unfolding
and they whispered to me:

Joy, joy.

Lilka Trzcinska-Croydon

Sorrow

Should we praise sorrow?

We aren't allowed to forget sorrow.
Dark phantoms rising
in the midst of a joyous moment
as we uphold a rose in full bloom.
Sorrow in its very essence,
its petals as momentary and fragile
as tears falling into silence.
Or early morning's bird song
keening sadly in linden's branches.
The mourning dove knows it too.

Oh my beloved,
we are suspended between
the warm security of oatmeal porridge
and a sharp blade of impending loss.

Sorrow will always be with us.
Should we praise sorrow?
Would we be able to see the joyful
twinkle of stars without
the darkness of night skies?
Should we praise dark skies?

And what about the bough
always in danger of breaking,
the cradle falling, falling
into ineffable dread?
Should we place the cradle
on the solid ground?
What if the ground opens up
and devours the cradle, baby and all?

We live in the sea of ashes
dark columns of smoke soaring, soaring,
mounds of ashes covering
white daisies in the fields.
Our words, barely audible, emerge
and rise above the sea.
Transformed into white doves
they circle the earth looking for an olive tree.

Tell me, should we praise sorrow?
Yes, for it is a bitter balm
for the heart broken by loss.
It dwells in the fallen star.
It also dwelled in the heart of one
who, liberated from the death camp,
was unable to see the faces of her liberators
for tears of sorrow clouded her eyes.
Tears of sorrow, for those who perished
before this day of resurrection,
were more powerful than tears of joy.

Mourning

> *I'll mourn always — you hear me? — for you*
> *alone, in Paradise.*
> Odysseas Elitis, "The Monogram"

Heather meadow in Kampinos forest,
cobalt-blue sky of autumn.
Our hearts on fire—we didn't know
a few months later we'd meet
on the main street of Auschwitz
where you, a twenty-one-year-old youth,
a prisoner in the men's camp,
waited for my Komando to pass by.
I, barely able to walk, my body on fire with **typhus**.
You, tall and handsome even in that prison **garb**.

It was easier to bear vermin, filth and cold,
illness, terrible hunger, even the loss of freedom:
in my heart I was free—you were close by,
Birkenau to Auschwitz just a bit farther
than Marszalkowska to Krucza Street in Warsaw.

Awareness of your closeness sustained, enlivened me.
Eyes scanning grim columns of prisoners
always searching for you.
Wooden clogs seemed light, empty stomach **felt full**,
my heart filled with tender love for you.

It is hard to mourn you
your death—a mere assumption.
These past fifty years nourished by hope
unreasonable, unfounded, destructive.

I'm writing my days—a tree shedding its leaves.
Carried by the wind they cover the heather **meadow**
while cobalt-blue skies look down, forever.

Sandee Gertz Umbach

The Bra Factory

I try to tell my brother
not to call himself a "go-fer"
just because he fetches snaps and cardboard
for women who say
"Bring me a double order,"
they get paid by the piece.

A thin vibration against her machine,
Wendy filled 40D cups
with soft paper and longing
until opting for a little more herself.
Jim hands her the most boxes,
her body buckling under the weight,
Wendy is the quietest 36C
I've ever known,
she can wear a skin tight mini with a halter
and never make a sound.

Her high breathless voice makes no impact,
among the carping yells—
the broads she's stacked up against,
the ones who have stuffed bras
for 22 years,
supporting alcoholic husbands
with a snap of their wrists,
as simple as taking off
an underwire, long before
we knew about carpal tunnel.

My brother says Wendy
gets a hard time about her clothes
what she reveals in a windowless room of lines—
about her boyfriend of 18 years,
how they'll get married
when he gets a steady job,
why she lives at home,

why he lives with his mother,
why they've gone on dates
while six presidents have come and gone
in the White House
and they still say goodnight at the door.

My brother keeps running,
says yes to Wendy
and the other pleading eyes,
moving too fast to speak
above the conveyor —
each repetition buys college,
clothes, a hip replacement.
My brother brings back tags and boxes
stacked to his temples
ones he knows will be left
untouched at day's end.
It's better than the hobby store —
13 years on a loading dock
till the notice —
this is the union
and it's harder to lose a job here,
racing around, supplying the women.

Once I asked him how they piece together
fabric and silk, thinking I could gain some insight
into American ingenuity and was surprised
to find out the bras really fly in from China.
They come in on crates, bows and snaps
already sewn — loading dock men
in Levi's and steel-toed boots
pry open the wooden folds,
dangle the first four or so,
hold up lace and satin
while women wait with "Lily of France" tags
pressed in the creases of raw, bent hands.

'Panasomu' People

*In Rusyn Language, meaning:
  people like us*

In fog of their magic forests,
the Carpathian Mountain people
laid low in their dirt beds
formed a barrier between countries—
a Hungarian king who hypnotized
them into silence, revolutions hollow
and long as a werewolf's call
and then stillness, and still no food.

One million people forced from their villages
of *Sucha* and *Lemko*, dispersed,
until their neighbor became Polish
their past forgotten rapes and beatings.
30,000 of them sit down to dinner
in Western Pennsylvania, bless hams
and answer grandchildren's questions;
"Who are we?", "Where do we come from?"
with *"Slovak, Ukrainian, Russian…"*

Those were the only choices the soldiers offered,
knocking at the straw mats
of Carpathian shacks,
in search of something they could
write in their shuffling papers.
"We are Rusyn!", they sang,
slap happy serfs in their Byzantine
aprons and brocaded collars,

➤

they were slaves but they knew
who they were—Rusyns who crooned
the clear sweet notes of their national anthem,
one soul wound into the tight strings of zithers
played after days spent sheaving
wheat, carrying stalks to priests
who might find favor in a son.

A people still afraid of the wind,
the night's howling,
and the evil red eye—
the village sleeps in turns,
one man asleep, one fanning
the russet flames of fires
leaping from their black
beautiful wood.

Wendy Visser

Leaf-scattered day
in her lap the family album.
Nameless faces

f.ward

in spite of all those taxes

    for my father
    April 30, 1933 to January 14, 1999

i saw that look of panic
in your eyes
before you had a chance
to hide it
you wanted us to think
you feared nothing
so you turned away
as we waited for the ambulance
then refused the stretcher
insisted on walking
while your heart was failing
and when we got there
you laughed so loud
from that hospital bed
flirting with the nurses
i'm sure they could hear you
on the other side
the maternity wing
propped up like a king
in his throne
you told the doctors
what to do next
having read all the books
you argued in the face of death
as though it was just a matter
of being the one in control
once again

you sent us all home

and when i got the call
to return
to that narrow bed
behind flesh pink curtain
drawn for privacy at least
they had no beds left
in the cardiac ward
in spite of all those taxes
you complained about paying
i was too late
time of death;
9:10pm
time on my underground parking ticket;
9:33pm
you always hated it
when people were late
looking so much smaller
but still warm
a thick plastic tube
jutting out of your mouth
undignified
but left there
for the coroner's benefit
they explain

you would not have approved

what do i do with all his stuff?
mom cried
and i knew what she meant
though the doctor looked confused

it all seems like
nothing, now
with you rolled out flat
staring at some strange ceiling
in the last bed in a row
in the hospital ER

a big black period at the end of
the sentence

while a nurse cuts a lock of your hair
for my mother
i look out the window

you chose the worst day for this

i don't think we've ever had
so much snow

Patricia Wellingham-Jones

Flatlanders Head for the Hills

The '51 Studebaker cranked around hair-pin turns,
swooped through crossings, out-ran stray dogs.
Father clutched the wheel, blue eyes blazing.
Mother, pale beside him, clucked her tongue.
Bottoms bounced, rough-fibered seat
rubbed red patches on tan bare skin.

My sister and I peered through open windows'
rushing air at ambling cows, valley lakes and peaks.
Shrilled our excitement
in Father's overwrought ear.
Mother wrung thin hands, moaned soft and low.

We roared through Adirondacks
to our cousins' country home,
left a few feathers in our wake.
Final flourish of the wheel,
brakes shrieked inches from the door.

Father swaggered, Mother staggered from the car.
Amply impressed, my uncle asked,
When did you get your license, Norm?
Father beamed in modest pride,
I've had it one whole week.

A.Z. Wells

From Suffering into Laughter

it is said that ravens bear
        the souls of the dead

so many ravens
haunt this settled shore
mischief angels
black laughing poltergeists
        taunting us
as we step through our doors
into blinding cold
        forgetful

        a drowned boy's hair floats
            spreads across the water
                like black-feathered wings
            another raven born from
        suffering into laughter

Iqaluit

Joanna M. Weston

    he carries
    grandfather's ashes
    boxed in his hands
        one man's history
        made small

Patience Wheatley

In an Old Limestone House at Belleville

we keep
the flowered curtain drawn
against cold

pull back the curtain
so I can see the starlight

all the dark misery
of old stones gathers
between these walls
where winter hoarfrost once
whitened the corners
and women with water-wrinkled hands
laboured under quilts that were histories of families
got and delivered children
every particle of beauty in their faces
dried up by red hot stoves
and terror
of winter homelessness

I need
to look out at old starlight
to see the world spinning forward

Sheila Windsor

haiku sequence

old manor house
each empty room has
its own echo

auction day...
in the heart-shaped locket
a faded soldier

dusk...
a white rose petals
the lawn

wild geese
how the long shadows
linger

attic bedroom
one small spider crosses
the moon

haiku sequence

there!
beneath dead leaves
snowdrops

forgotten squeak
dad's old wheelbarrow
along the path

almost time
to scent the summer air
white lilac...

first barefoot
day of the year
touching base

windows and doors
thrown open

Elana Wolff

The Way to Make a Mask

After April in Ypres, the mask
assumes a meta-meaning
              keenly tied to life.

Realistic models
of these World War One exemplars
can be easily
reproduced by folks at home:
Take a rag.
Urinate on it.
Hold it over your nose and breathe.

Remember, April is the month of lilacs.

Margaret Malloch Zielinski

Mallory

Mallory disappeared on the slopes of Everest on June 8, 1924. His body was discovered on May 1, 1999.

Flexed fingers clawing
the frozen gravel,
you cling for a lifetime
to the peak.

Your muscled shoulders
covered still in the smooth
and fleshy skin of youth,
your back, wide, made strong

by years of climbing.
On the bare mountain side,
your pelvic bones stand out,
white wounds

amongst the stones and rock.
Himalayan blizzards long ago blasted
your wool, your tweeds.. Only a tangle
of rope, shreds of leather, remain.

Goggles, a box of Swan Vesta matches,
nail scissors and a safety pin
lie among the gravel
and round your neck,

a leather pouch stuffed with letters.
How close you were to success,
how loyal to your companion, Irvine,
the snapped rope around your waist

testifying you climbed together
until your fall to death
—and glory. Was it worth
all those lost years:

your children laughing, flying
high on the swing you'd hung
from the apple tree—swinging
low and scraping their toes

through the gravel, that shifts—
like the stones you cling to now
and forever alone in the clouds
—so close to heaven?

Lizzie

She looks so young, my grandmother,
smooth rounded cheeks,
frizzy hair pulled back, tight.
But wavy strands escape
into a halo around her head.
On her knee, her plump baby's
lace trimmed bodice
matches the flounces of his mother's lacy collar,
though she is stiff, so tightly
corseted beneath her black dress.

I pray the years after were blessed
with children's sticky hugs,
laughter under the chestnut tree,
humming-birds and honeysuckle,
hot crusty bread
each morning from the baker on Mill Street,
gossip with Kirsty McKenzie,
afternoon tea in the lilac shade,
loving nights with John
curtained close in the soft boxbed.

For I knew only a fat old woman
bulging in her shiny black dress,
legs swollen, unsteady,
white hair still frizzy,
widowed and unwillingly invited
to live alone in our cold front parlour,
to eat alone, dip biscuits in her tea,
sit silently,
stare bewildered through the window
at the gray sea.

Notes on the Poets

Becky D. Alexander — Cambridge, Ontario — won an honourable mention, as judged by Denver Stull, in the 2000 Herb Barrett Award contest for her "riding the grapevine" and another honourable mention in the 2001 Milton Acorn Prize for Poetry contest. She has published both poetry and prose and has four titles to her credit: *On Raven's Wings, Down Hammett's Lane, Lost Boots*, and, most recently, *Days the Willows Choose*. Becky has work in all ten volumes of *Writers Undercover*. She edited the haiku anthology *Paradise Poems* for hamilton haiku press in 1998. Becky is the founder of Craigleigh Press. In 2002 the City of Cambridge presented her with its Bernice Adams Cultural Award.

Kristin Andrychuk — Kingston, Ontario — was born in Kirkland Lake and grew up on the Niagara Peninsula. She is the author of the novels *The Swing Tree* and *Riding the Comet*. Her short stories have appeared in anthologies such as the annual *Best Canadian Stories* (1991) and *Flash Fiction*.

Tammy Armstrong — Halifax, Nova Scotia — won the Alfred Bailey Prize for Poetry in 2000 and the David Adams Richards Prize in 1999. She placed third in the 2000 National Poetry Contest of the League of Canadian Poets.

Winona Baker — Nanaimo, British Columbia — won an honourable mention, as judged by Margaret Saunders, in the 1997 Herb Barrett Award contest for her haiku "horse's muzzle." She also won third prize in the 1999 Tidepool Prize for Poetry contest. Winona is the author of several collections of haiku and longer poems including *Clouds Empty Themselves: Island Haiku, Not So Scarlet a Woman: Light and Humorous Poems, Moss-hung Trees: Haiku of the West Coast, Beyond the Lighthouse, Wild Strawberries*, and, most recently, *Even a Stone Breathes*. Her poetry has appeared in over 70 anthologies and has been translated into five languages

David Barnett — Pencader, Wales — is the author of *The Mask of Siam, Bent in Water, Fretwork*, and *All the Year Round*. He generally lives in a remote farmhouse on the edge of the moorland in West Wales, where he's part of an amazing community, but he sometimes can be found in the foothills of Andalucia.

Jacqueline Bartlett — Heswall, England — was born in Nottinghamshire to parents who were both writers. In addition to her poetry, she has written short fiction and radio plays. Jacqueline's poetry has appeared in anthologies such as *Making Worlds: 100 Contemporary Women Poets*. She is Warden of the Quaker Meeting House on the Wirral (near Liverpool).

Theda Bassett — Murray, Utah — was born in Afton, Wyoming. She worked for the telephone company and the US Postal Service, retiring as a public affairs specialist from the Bureau of Reclamation in 1987. Her books include *Grandpa Neibaur Was a Pioneer* and *Writing Between the Lines*. Her poetry has appeared in several prize anthologies, including books by the poetry societies of Pennsylvania, Georgia, Kentucky, and Utah, and the National Federation of State Poetry Societies. She has three sons, a daughter, and 16 grandchildren.

Catherine Bayne — Godfrey, Ontario — was born in **New Jersey** and moved to Canada at age seven. She has published haiku in the annual anthologies of Haiku Canada. "The Elm" is her first non-haiku poem to be published.

Marion Beck — Regina, Saskatchewan — was born in Rossendale, England, and graduated in geography from Leeds University. She is the author of six poetry collections: *Notebook of an Immigrant, Thin Grafts, Counting the Threads, Poems for Amazons, Trench in the Rockies,* and *DRY is the long term forecast.* Marion won the Short Grain Prose Poem Contest in 1991 and is a double winner of the People's Political Poem Contest. In terms of non-fiction, she has published articles on autistic children in the U.K. and the U.S.

Roger Bell — Port McNicoll, Ontario — see page 177.

Patricia M. Benedict — Calgary, Alberta — won second prize, as judged by Denver Stull, in the 2000 Herb Barrett Award contest for her "Lop-sided swing." She was born in Dublin, Ireland and came to Canada in the 1970s. Patricia was a university teacher for 20 years before her retirement in 1996. Since then she has received an honourable mention in the Betty Drevniok Award haiku contest.

Paul Berry — King's Lynn, England — has five poetry collections to his credit: *Homages and Holiday Snaps, A Bequest of Fire, Earth Musk* and *Country Dark, Legacies,* and *The Cries of Ashes.* He also is the author of the social history, *Airfield Heyday.* Paul served as editor of *Poet's England: Norfolk,* the county he lives in with wife and two sons.

Izak Bouwer — Ottawa, Ontario — won an honourable mention, as judged by Michael Dylan Welch, in the 1998 Herb Barrett Award contest for his haiku "longer days." He and his wife Dina are ex-South Africans. Izak is a retired mathematics professor interested in haiku, Zen, and the Japanese language. In Fredericton, N.B., they helped run a weekly workshop on the art and poetry of William Blake. He also writes fiction and his novella, *The Vertebrae of a Long Snake,* was published in the *Mike Shayne Mystery Magazine* (January, 1985).

Ronnie R. Brown — Ottawa, Ontario — won first prize, as judged by Al Purdy, in the 1977 Sandburg-Livesay Anthology Contest for her poem "Photographs That Should Have Been Taken." She also won first prize in the 1999 Tidepool Prize for Poetry contest and second prize in the 2001 Tidepool Prize for Poetry contest. She took third prize as well as an honourable mention in the 2000 Orion Prize for Poetry contest and an honourable mention in the 2000 Milton Acorn Prize for Poetry contest. Ronnie is the author of three poetry collections: *Re Creation, Decisive Moments,* and *Photographic Evidence* (shortlisted for the Archibald Lampman Award). A fourth collection, *States of Matter,* is on its way from Black Moss Press.

Brian Burke — Vancouver, British Columbia — won second prize in the 2002 Tidepool Prize for Poetry contest. His chapbook is *margaret atwood island* and his short fiction has appeared in *Stag Line: Stories by Men* (Coteau Books).

Anita Gevaudan Byerly — Pittsburgh, Pennsylvania — is the author of one collection: *Digging a Hole to China.* She won the *In Pittsburgh* Newsweekly Poetry

Competition In 1987. Anita has also been a finalist or semifinalist for the poetry awards offered by *Negative Capability, Comstock Review*, and *yawp*. She has been nominated for the 2004 Mary Roberts Rinehart Poetry Award.

Terry Ann Carter — Nepean, Ontario — was born in Cambridge, Massachusetts. She will participate in the next Bashō Festival in Japan. Her poetry collection is *Waiting for Julia*.

Denise Coney — Newmarket, Ontario — served as co-editor of the haiku journal *Inkstone*. Her own haiku have appeared in several anthologies, such as *Haiku Moment* and *Milkweed*. Denise is a social worker who enjoys hiking on the Ganaraska Trail.

Gloe Cormie — Winnipeg, Manitoba — teaches creative writing and creative expression in the schools. She has won literary awards from *Prairie Fire, Contemporary Verse 2*, and *People's Poetry*. Gloe's work has been broadcast nationally on CBC radio, and is widely anthologized. Gloe's poetry book, *Sea Salt, Red Oven Mitts and the Blues*, was shortlisted for the Eileen McTavish Sykes Award.

Terrance Cox — St. Catharines, Ontario — is the author of the prize-winning book *Radio & Other Miracles* and *Local Scores*, a CD combining spoken word with music. He won the 2002 Niagara Book Prize. Terrance teaches arts and humanities at Brock University. He is also associate editor and music columnist for *Niagara Current*.

Barbara Ruth Crupi — Frating, Nr. Colchester, England — was born in Suffolk. She has always been interested in nature and the countryside, and has lived on a farm in Essex for 30 years but no longer farms. She began composing poetry as a child, originally to please an invalid grandmother, and soon won prizes and local publication, but as an adult only began submitting and publishing poetry after her two grown daughters left home. She also writes short stories and sketches. Her collections are *Shadow Chasing, The Well Pool,* and *Before the Winter Comes*.

Ernest Dewhurst — Lathom, England — had a farm childhood in the Pennines. His two poetry collections are *A Hint of Hedgerows* and *Lantern in the Lane*. He is a founding member of the Inklings, a Liverpool writers' group. Ernest's chief interests are family, countryside, people, writing, and church work.

John Dixon — Neston, England — is a now-retired second-generation veterinarian. His published writing is nearly all technical, and devoted to immunity and parasitism. John lives in an 18th-century house overlooking the Dee Valley and North Wales. His verse is often driven by frustration, chiefly with the unadmitted failure of modern, secular thinking.

Fay Eagle — Prenton, United Kingdom — was brought up in Yorkshire, and trained as a nurse and midwife. She worked in Australia and New Zealand before returning to England. Her poetry book is *Journey into a Landscape*. Fay's poetry is included in *Poet's England: Cheshire* and *Poet's England: Derbyshire*, and has received radio broadcast.

Gerald England — Hyde, England — is the author of *A Poetic Sequence for Five Voices, Mousings, The Wine the Women and the Song, For Her Volume One, Meetings at the Moor's Edge, The Rainbow and Other Poems, Daddycation, Futures* (with Christine England), *Stealing Kisses, Four Square Replay,* and *Limbo Time.* He has also edited several books, most recently, *The Art of Haiku 2000.* He lives on the edge of the Pennines and has been active in the British small press scene for over 35 years.

Janice M. Faria — Pittsburgh, Pennsylvania — works at the Women's Center and Shelter of Greater Pittsburgh. She has been involved with the Carlow College Creative Writing Program, the Pittsburgh Poetry Exchange, and the Pittsburgh Center for the Arts.

Rina Ferrarelli — Pittsburgh, Pennsylvania — was born in Italy and came to the US at the age of fifteen. She won second prize, as judged by Raymond Souster, in the 1999 Sandburg-Livesay Anthology Contest for her poem "The Swifts." She also won an honourable mention in the 2000 Milton Acorn Prize for Poetry contest. She has two poetry collections to her credit: *Home Is a Foreign Country* and *Dreamsearch*. Rina has also translated two volumes from the Italian: *I Saw the Muses* (by Giorgio Chesura) and *Light Without Motion* (by Leonardo Sinisgalli), and has won the Italo Calvino Prize from the Columbia University Translation Center. Her work has been included in many anthologies, most recently *Kindled Terraces: American Poets in Greece.*

Linda Frank — Hamilton, Ontario — grew up in Montreal, moving to Hamilton in 1977. She is the author of four poetry collections: *Taste the Silence,* *...It Takes A Train To Cry, Orpheus Descending,* and *Cobalt Moon Embrace*. Linda serves on the executive of the Hamilton Poetry Centre and presently teaches social science at Mohawk College.

Michael Fraser — Toronto, Ontario — was born in Grenada, and has lived in Canada since the age of five. Currently he teaches school in Toronto. Michael is the editor of *Sapodilla*. His work has appeared in the anthology *Seed*.

Ann Goldring — Stouffville, Ontario — won an honourable mention, as judged by Raymond Souster, in the 1999 Sandburg-Livesay Anthology Contest for her haiku "among marigolds." She also won an honourable mention, as judged by Margaret Saunders, in the 1997 Herb Barrett Award contest for her haiku "on my knees." Her junior novel, *Spitfire,* was published in 2001. Ann is a founding member of Haiku Deer Park and she is active in Haiku Canada.

Alistair Halden — Aberfeldy, Scotland — has three collections to his credit: *At the Cliff Edge, It Is Hard To Explain,* and *To Travel Hopefully*. He and his wife live in the Central Highlands, overlooking Loch Tay. Alistair also writes crime novels and is interested in church, gardening, and tennis.

Irene Blair Honeycutt — Charlotte, North Carolina — is the author of *It Comes as a Dark Surprise*, which won the New South Poetry Series Contest. She teaches creative writing at Central Piedmont Community College.

Sheila Hyland — Toronto, Ontario — is originally from England. She is the author of the collections *On Grenadier Pond, Love Lines, A Given Line, Misty*

Willows, Spring Season, Summer Season, For Autumn, and *Wintersong*. She has edited *Strong Winds* for the Canadian Poetry Association and a haiku anthology, *One Day in the Life of the Valley*, forthcoming from hamilton haiku press. Sheila's poems are published internationally and have received radio broadcast.

Ellen S. Jaffe — Hamilton, Ontario — won first prize as well as an honourable mention in the 2000 Orion Prize for Poetry contest. She grew up in New York, studied in England, and has lived in Ontario since 1979. Anthology appearances include *Intricate Countries: women poets from earth to sky, Apparitions: visions of the millennium,* and *After the Eclipse*. She has twice won book awards from Arts Hamilton, once for her poetry collection *Water Children* and again for her non-fiction title *Writing Your Way*. Ellen co-organized Hamilton's Celebration of Jewish Writers and Writing.

Hans Jongman — Toronto, Ontario — won third prize, as judged by Denver Stull, in the 2000 Herb Barrett Award contest for his "deertracks." He was born in The Hague and came to Canada from the Netherlands in 1969 after having worked as a sailor. He is a member of the Canadian Association for the Advancement of Netherlandic Studies. Hans has served as membership secretary of Haiku Canada for the past six years. Hans edited the haiku anthology *Sweeping Leaves* for hamilton haiku press. His own poems have appeared in over twenty anthologies, most recently *Tulip Haiku*, Shoreline, 2004.

Kristine Kaposy lives in Montreal, Quebec.

Earl R. Keener — Bethany, West Virginia — works on the track gang at Weirton Steel.

Philomene Kocher — Kingston, Ontario — is co-author (with Marco Fraticelli) of the septenga collection *The Second Time*. Her other chief interest in photography.

Ken Kowal — Winnipeg, Manitoba — won an honourable mention in the 2000 Milton Acorn Prize for Poetry contest. He is the author of two collections: *i dream my father's hands* and *Brookside Poems*.

David P. Kozinski lives in Wilmington, Delaware.

Joan Latchford — Toronto, Ontario — was born in 1926 but did not begin writing until 1993. She publishes chapbooks under her Micro Prose imprint. She is a noted photographer. Her poetry chapbooks are *Pearly Gates and other separations* and *The Streets Where I Live*.

John B. Lee — Brantford, Ontario — grew up on a farm in Highgate, Ontario. He won an honourable mention, as judged by Raymond Souster, in the 1999 Sandburg-Livesay Anthology Contest for his poem "The Dog Who Died in the Dark." John is the only double winner of the Milton Acorn Memorial People's Poetry Award (now the Acorn-Plantos Award), 1993 & 1995. He has also won the Tilden Canadian Literary Award in 1995. In 1996 he won the People's Poetry Award and in 1997 the People's Political Poem Award. His collections of poetry are *Poems Only A Dog Could Love, Love Among the Tombstones, To Kill a White Dog, Fossils of the Twentieth Century, Hired Hands, Small Worlds, The Day Jane Fonda Came to Guelph, Rediscovered Sheep, The Bad Philosophy of Good Cows,*

The Pig Dance Dreams, The Hockey Player Sonnets, When Shaving Seems Like Suicide, Variations on Herb, The Art of Walking Backwards, All the Cats Are Gone, These Are the Days of Dogs and Horses, The Beatles Landed Laughing in New York, Tongues of the Children, In a Language with No Word for Horses, Never Hand Me Anything if I Am Walking or Standing, Soldier's Heart, The Echo of Your Words Has Reached Me, Stella's Journey, Don't Be So Persnickety (poems for children), *An Almost Silent Drumming: The South African Poems, The Half-Way Tree, In the Terrible Weather of Guns, Totally Unused Heart, Though Their Joined Hearts Drummed Like Larks,* and *The Bright Red Apples of the Dead.* In addition, John has four non-fiction books to his credit, and he has edited or co-edited seven anthologies, all out from Black Moss Press.

Anne Lewis-Smith — Newport, Dyfed, Wales — served for over fifty years as editor of many magazines, including *Envoi,* and as managing director of Envoi Poets Publications. She has now retired from editing others' work to concentrate on her own, and has several poetry books in print. Anne is a balloonist with over thirty years' experience, a grandmother, an inveterate scribbler, and a lover of islands.

Noah Leznoff — Markham, Ontario — is the author of two poetry books: *Why We Go To Zoos* and *Outside Magic.* He teaches English, philosophy, and creative writing at Unionville High School.

Robert Lima — State College, Pennsylvania — is the author of 22 books of poetry, critical studies, drama, and biography. His works include *The Theatre of García Lorca; Borges the Labyrinth Maker; Ramón del Valle-Inclán; Dos ensayos sobre teatro español de los veinte; Valle-Inclán, The Theatre of His Life; The Dramatic World of Valle-Inclán; Dark Prisms, Occultism in Hispanic Drama; Valle-Inclán, El teatro de su vida;* as well as seven volumes of poetry: *Poems of Exile and Alienation; Fathoms; Corporal Works; The Olde Ground; Mayaland; Sardinia/Sardegna;* and *Tracking the Minotaur.* Dr. Lima is Professor Emeritus of Spanish and Comparative Literature at Pennsylvania State University. He has been elected Academician of the Academia Norteamericana de la Lengua Eapañola and Corresponding Member of Spain's Real Academia de la Lengua. Prof. Lima has received many honours, among them membership in the Enxebre Orden da Vieira, and he has been knighted and received into the Order of Queen Isabel of Spain.

Norma West Linder — Sarnia, Ontario — was born in Toronto but spent her formative years on Manitoulin Island. She won second prize in the 1999 Tidepool Prize for Poetry contest. She is the author of five novels. Her short stories have been published internationally in anthologies and journals and broadcast on the CBC. Norma's nine volumes of poetry are *On the Side of the Angels, Pyramid, Ring Around the Sun, The Rooming House, This Age of Reason, Matter of Life and Death, Morning Child, River of Lethe,* and *Jazz in the Old Orange Hall.* She has also written a memoir of Manitoulin Island, a children's book, and a biography of Pauline McGibbon. Before retirement, she taught at Lambton College for 24 years.

Mikal Lofgren — Salt Lake City, Utah — was born and raised in Idaho Falls, Idaho. His book *Trudi Smiles Back* won the Utah State Poetry Society prize in

1998. His poem "Silver" took first prize in the *Poet's Market 2000* contest. Mikal retired from the Salt Lake City Fire Department to devote his time to writing. In 1998 he was named Utah's Poet of the Year.

Robin Lovell — Toronto, Ontario — was born in England and moved to Canada in the late 1950s. For many years he was an accountant. His work has appeared in several anthologies including *Sweeping Leaves* and *Prairie Sunset* (both from hamilton haiku press), *Handprints on the Future*, and *Poetry for Painters*. Robin died after entering these haiku.

Neil mac Neil — Murcia, Spain — is from Scotland, but moved to Spain last year. He writes and publishes in both Scots and English. His poetry is widely published in books and anthologies. These include *Poems 1960–1970, Clydesmoke, The Catcha Bus Blues, Timescales, Night Dreams of Nailloran, After the Watergaw, Present Poets 2, Old Songs Getting Younger, An Intimate City, Smile the Weird Joy, Variations on a New Song*, and *Fox in the Heather*. In 1989 Neil won the Scottish International Open Poetry Competition and in 1974 the Alice Gregory Memorial Prize (long poem). He is a fellow of the Institute of Contemporary Scotland.

Giovanni Malito — Cork, Ireland — was born in Toronto to parents from Calabria, Italy. He held a Ph.D. in chemistry from the U. of T., and was a post-doctoral fellow at the University of Strasbourg in France. Giovanni lived in Ireland with his wife and children for the last decade of his life. He won first prize, as judged by Margaret Saunders, in the 1997 Herb Barrett Award contest for his haiku "cold morning." A literary dynamo, he published well over 4000 poems in literary magazines in two dozen nations and in seven languages around the world. His own publications are *Touching the Moon, Notes of a Physics Teacher, Why I Don't Read Newspapers, Unnatural Science, To Be the Fourth Wise Man, Animal Crackers, Slingshot, Voglio, A Poet's Manifesto, Word Sonnets, Spreading Ashes, Treading Water*, and *Misleads*. He was the founder and editor/publisher of *The Brobdingnagian Times*. Giovanni Malito died of cancer last year at the age of 46.

Joy Hewitt Mann — Spencerville, Ontario — won third prize, as judged by Raymond Souster, in the 1999 Sandburg-Livesay Anthology Contest for her poem "The Simplicity of Believers." That same year Joy won the Acorn-Rukeyser Chapbook Contest for *grass*. She also won first prize in the 2001 Tidepool Prize for Poetry contest, third prize in the 2002 Milton Acorn Prize for Poetry contest, and third prize in the 2000 Tidepool Prize for Poetry contest. In addition to *grass*, Joy's other poetry collection is *Voices From the Other Side of the Moon*. She has also published *Clinging to Water*, a short story collection. She runs a book & collectibles shop.

John E. Marks — Manchester, England — is a tutor at The Open University and a cricket fan. He has had articles on Hardy's and Hopkins' poetry published. John's collections are *Soundbites, Lifting the Veil*, and *Thinking Allowed*.

Ben Murray — Edmonton, Alberta — won first prize in the Canadian Poetry Association Poetry Awards. He was a finalist for both the Acorn-Rukeyser Chapbook and Ralph Gustafson Poetry Prizes. Ben is also a musician.

Sue Nevill — Vancouver, British Columbia — was born in England. She has a typically eclectic background: jobs in advertising, archaeological mudpits, bars, berry fields, bookshops; travels in Europe, the Mediterranean, and the Caribbean; obsessions from baseball to opera, geology to jazz. She supports her poetry habit through freelance writing and flea markets and is taking humanities courses at Simon Fraser University. Her books are *I was expecting someone taller* and *All You Expect of the Road*.

Renee Norman — Coquitlam, British Columbia — is the author of *House of Mirrors*. She holds a Ph.D. from U.B.C., and lives and teaches in Coquitlam. Her poems and short stories have been published in journals and newspapers.

H.F. Noyes — Politia, Attikis, Greece — won the Haiku Society of America's Sora Award in 2004. He is the author of *My Rain, My Moon; Star Carvings; The Blossoming Rudder; Just Floating Here; The Moment's Gift; Oar Under Water; Between Two Waves;* and *still here* (from which the poems in this volume are taken). He has also published five volumes of *Favorite Haiku* (haiku, commentary, and essays). He is a native of Oregon who practised psychotherapy in New York for a quarter-century before moving to Greece.

Anne-Marie Oomen — Empire, Michigan — is Chairwoman of the Creative Writing Department at the Interlochen Arts Academy. She also serves as staff assistant at the Stonecoast Writers Conference, University of Southern Maine. Anne-Marie has two poetry chapbooks to her credit as well as anthology appearances. She is the founding editor of *Dunes Review,* and her two cats are named Walt Whitman and Emily Dickinson.

Kathy Pearce-Lewis — Ra'anana, Israel — was born in New York, raised in Colorado, and lived in Maryland. She is a linguist and a member of The Writer's Center. Her poems have appeared in several anthologies such as *Rye Bread, Weavings 2000,* and *Autumn Harvest*. She is a member of Voices Israel.

Linda Vigen Phillips — Charlotte, North Carolina — teaches elementary school (full-time) and writing for children courses at Queens University (part-time). She recently developed curriculum for Alliant Energy, Clear Channel's *The Human Genome,* and the Audubon Society.

Marilyn Gear Pilling — Hamilton, Ontario — see page 178.

Peggy Poole — West Kirby, England — was born on a farm in Kent. She won first prize, as judged by Jim C. Wilson, in the 1998 Sandburg-Livesay Anthology Contest for her poem "Sentences." Her poetry publications are *Never a Put-up Job, Cherry Stones and Other Poems, No Wilderness in Them, Midnight Walk, Hesitations, Trusting the Rainbow, Bruised, Rich Pickings, At the Tide's Edge, Polishing Pans,* and, most recently, *Selected Poems*. Peggy has edited several anthologies including *Poet's England: Cumbria*. She runs poetry courses and tutors for the *Writers News* Home Study poetry course.

Al Purdy — Ameliasburg, Ontario — won the Governor General's Award for Poetry twice (1965 and 1986). He also won the Milton Acorn Memorial People's Poetry Award (now the Acorn-Plantos Award) in 1991. In 1983 Al was appointed to the Order of Canada and his appointment to the Order of Ontario came in 1987. His 33 volumes of poetry won many other awards and prizes. His books are *The Enchanted Echo; Pressed on Sand; Emu, Remember!; The Crafte So Long to Lerne; The Blur in Between; Poems for All the Annettes; The Cariboo Horses; North of Summer: Poems from Baffin Island; Wild Grape Wine; Love in a Burning Building; The Quest for Ouzo; Hiroshima Poems; Selected Poems; On the Bearpaw Sea; Sex and Death; In Search of Owen Roblin; The Poems of Al Purdy; Sundance at Dusk; A Handful of Earth; At Marsport Drugstore; Moths in the Iron Curtain; No Second Spring; Being Alive; The Stone Bird; Birdwatching at the Equator: The Galapagos Islands; Bursting into Song; Piling Blood; The Collected Poems of Al Purdy; The Woman on the Shore; Naked With Summer in Your Mouth; Rooms for Rent in the Outer Planets; To Paris Never Again;* and *Beyond Remembering.* He also published 11 non-poetry books (letters, criticism, and a novel) and edited three major anthologies of Canadian poetry. Al Purdy died shortly after entering this contest. Charles Bukowski called him "one of the few very good poets since 1900."

Gina Riley — Maghull, England — was born and educated in Liverpool. Her anthology *Spirit Levels* was published by The National Poetry Foundation. Her poetry has appeared in anthologies such as *New Christian Poetry* and *Poet's England: Wirral.* Gina was joint-winner in the written section of *Poetry Digest's* Bard of the Year competition.

Lynn Veach Sadler — Sanford, North Carolina — won third prize in the 2001 Orion Prize for Poetry contest. Among her other awards are the Sara Henderson Hay Prize from *The Pittsburgh Quarterly,* the Poetry Society of America's Hemly Award, the poetry prizes offered by *Asphodel* and *Kalliope,* and the Lee Witte Poetry Contest for her 2003 collection *Poet Geography.* Her other poetry collection is *Lynn Veach Sadler: Greatest Hits, 1995-2001.* She also writes short stories; her fiction has won awards from *Cream City Review, Rambunctious Review,* the North Carolina Writers' Network, and *Talus and Scree.* Dr. Sadler is the author of five academic books and 68 professional articles. She has also written plays, a libretto, and a novel.

Joanna Catherine Scott — Chapel Hill, North Carolina — won the 2000 Acorn-Rukeyser Chapbook Contest for *Coming Down From Bataan.* Among her other awards are the Capricorn Poetry Award, the *americas review* Prize for Social Poetry, the PEN/Nob Hill Poetry Award, the New England Prize for Poetry, the Blumenthal Award, and the North Carolina Poetry Society's Poet Laureate Award. Joanna was born in England and raised in Australia. In addition to *Coming Down from Bataan,* her poetry collections are *Breakfast at the Shangri-La* (winner of the Black Zinnias Award) and *Birth Mother* (winner of the Longleaf Poetry Award). She has published three prize-winning novels: *Cassandra, Lost; Charley and the Children;* and *The Lucky Gourd Shop.* Also to her credit are a bedroom farce and a volume of oral histories from Indochina. She holds a graduate degree in philosophy from Duke University.

Jeff Seffinga — Hamilton, Ontario — published his first poem in 1958 and he has never completely terminated his involvement with poetry in all its aspects. His poetry reflects his rural roots and a deep concern for man's responsibility to and for the natural world. He currently runs the Acorn-Plantos Award for People's Poetry. Jeff's seven poetry titles are *Three Crows Flying, Lunatic Hands, Tight Shorts, Bailey's Mill, a reststop along the infinite road, We Measure Our Time in Coffee Cups,* and *Garden Concert.*

Shirley A. Serviss — Edmonton, Alberta — has two poetry collections to her credit: *Model Families* and *Reading Between the Lines*. She also co-edited *Study in Grey*, an anthology on women and depression.

K.V. Skene — Cork, Ireland — has won the Shaunt Basmajian Chapbook Award twice, in 2002 for her manuscript *Only a Dragon* (which includes her poem in the present anthology) and in 2004 for *Calendar of Rain*. Her poetry collections also include *Pack Rat, fire water, The Uncertainty Factor/As a Rock, Elemental Mind*, and *The Arran Designs and other poems*. An expat Canadian, she has lived in England for many years, but is temporarily residing in Ireland.

Tammara Or Slilat — Lower Galilee, Israel — is the author of *Children Are Made Of Dream Matter* and *Only Love Can*. She is also a painter and has exhibited her work in Israel. In 2004 she won the Jordan Valley prize for art.

Marvin Smith — Cleveland, Ohio — operates the Marv Smith Studio featuring painting, printmaking, and pottery.

Raymond Souster — Toronto, Ontario — is the author of 51 poetry collections: *When We Are Young; Go to Sleep, World; City Hall Street; Shake Hands with the Hangman; A Dream that is Dying; Walking Death; For What Time Slays; The Selected Poems; Crêpe-Hangers Carnival; A Local Pride; Place of Meeting; At Split Rock Falls; The Colour of the Times* (which won the Governor General's Award); *12 New Poems; Ten Elephants on Yonge Street; As Is; Lost & Found; So Far So Good; The Years; Selected Poems of Raymond Souster; Change-Up; Double-Header; Rain-Check; Extra Innings; Hanging In; From Hell to Breakfast* (with Douglas Alcorn); *Collected Poems of Raymond Souster* (in 9 volumes, 1940-1995); *Going the Distance; Queen City* (with Bill Brooks); *Jubilee of Death; Into this dark earth* (with James Deahl); *Flight of the Roller Coaster; It Takes All Kinds; The Eyes of Love; Asking for More; Running Out the Clock; Riding the Long Black Horse; Old Bank Notes; No Sad Songs Wanted Here; Close to Home; Of Time & Toronto; Let's All Go To the Ballgame;* and *Twenty-Four New Poems*. He has also published two novels and a history of The League of Canadian Poets and has edited some fifteen anthologies, textbooks, and single-author volumes of poetry. In addition to the Governor General's Award, he has been awarded the Centennial Medal, the Canadian Silver Jubilee Medal, the City of Toronto Award, and the Order of Canada.

Margaret Speak — York, England — was the deviser and co-founder of the Yorkshire Open Poetry Competition, now in its 20th year. Her poetry and prose have won many competitions, including the Cardiff, Exeter, and Bridport Prizes. Margaret's work is widely anthologized in books such as *Making Worlds: 100 Contemporary Women Poets*.

Elizabeth St Jacques — Sault Ste. Marie, Ontario — won second prize, as judged by Margaret Saunders, in the 1997 Herb Barrett Award contest for her haiku "Spring break." A published writer for 35 years, her work has been published in ten countries. She is the author of eight books, including *Around the Tree of Light,* the first collection of original English-language sijo poetry published in North America. Her 1995 haiku collection, *A Dance of Light,* earned the Merit Book Award (Haiku Society of America), a 1995 Albatross Award

(Romania), and was among *Small Press Review's* November picks, 1995. She is associate editor of *Sijo West,* poetry editor of *Canadian Writer's Journal,* contributing editor of *Small Press Review,* and a book review editor with *Albatross.* She maintains two websites:
"Haiku Light" http://members.tripod.com/~Startag/HAIKULIGHTindex.html and "Sijo Blossoms" http://members.tripod.com/Startag/Sijo.html

Sandra Staas — Coraopolis, Pennsylvania — is a native of Scotland. She publishes widely in U.S. and British magazines. Sandra photographs and writes online photo tours, the links to which can be found at her website: www.weewindaes.com

Jean Stanbury — West Kirby, England — is of Scottish descent, and her love of Scotland is reflected in much of her poetry. In addition, some of her poems are about the cruelty, tragedy, and pity of war. Jean's work has been broadcast on the BBC and has been included in anthologies. She is the author of the collection *Winged Seeds.*

Valerie Stetson — Kelowna, British Columbia — won the Bronwen Wallace Memorial Award for short fiction in 2001. Her work has been in anthologies such as *Gifts: Poems for Parents* and *Running Barefoot: Women Write The Land.*

Sheila Stewart — Toronto, Ontario — won the *Pottersfield Portfolio* Annual Short Poem Contest (for "Ladybones," included in this volume) and the Scarborough Arts Council "Window on Words" Contest. Her poetry book is *A Hat to Stop a Train.* Sheila works on adult literacy issues.

Andrew Stickland — Cambridge, England — was born in Scotland and spent several years living and studying in both London and Jyväskylä, Finland. His three poetry collections are *Broken Bottles, The Opposite Page,* and *Mathematical Love.* Andrew is currently a freelance writer, editor, and journalist based in Cambridge.

Lynn Tait — Sarnia, Ontario — was born in Toronto. Her work has been included in anthologies such as *Henry's Creature: poems and stories on the automobile* and *Body Language.* In 1999 she took second place in the Prickly Poetry Contest. Her first collection is *Breaking Away.*

Adèle Kearns Thomas — Sarnia, Ontario — is the author of two poetry books: *Behind the Scenes* and *Scattered Perceptions.* She was born in Hull, Quebec, and was raised in the Gatineau Hills.

Carolyn Thomas — Carlsbad, California — is the author of *Drawing, Shadows and Light, basho's frog, Play of Forms, Nirvana, whistling, no wind, Wisdom of Circles   Wisdom of Stones, ordinary rain...,* and *puddle on the ink stone.* She's also an artist. Her work appears internationally.

Stephen Threlkeld — Hamilton, Ontario — grew up in Cornwall, England. After serving in the Royal Air Force he worked five years as a shepherd. He came to Canada in 1953 and was a professor of biology at McMaster University, specializing in genetics. Dr. Threlkeld's poems have appeared in several anthologies such as *Strong Winds, A Cliff Runs Through It,* and *This I Believe.*

Mildred Tremblay — Nanaimo, British Columbia — won an honourable mention in the 1999 Tidepool Prize for Poetry contest. Mildred also won the Poet of the Year competition in 1996 (*Arc* magazine) and the Orillia prize for humour. She is the author of *Old Woman Comes Out of Her Cave* (poetry) and *Dark Forms Gliding* (short stories).

Lilka Trzcinska-Croydon — Toronto, Ontario — won second prize in the 2001 Milton Acorn Prize for Poetry contest. She was born in Poland in 1925. She and her family were arrested by the Gestapo in 1943 for involvement in the Resistance. Her mother died in Auschwitz, but her father, brother, and two sisters survived. After liberation in 1945 from Bergen-Belsen, where she had been transferred, she went to Italy, and the next year to England. In 1948 she moved to Toronto. Lilka is a psychoanalytic child therapist in private practice. Lilka writes in both Polish and English; other interests include painting, travel, cinema, Greek drama, and mythology.

Sandee Gertz Umbach — Washington, Pennsylvania — won first prize, as judged by Raymond Souster, in the 1999 Sandburg-Livesay Anthology Contest for her poem "I Can't Help But Think About Eve." She is volunteer director and founder of the Washington Community Arts and Cultural Center, where she teaches poetry. Sandee's articles and essays have appeared in the *Pittsburgh Post-Gazette* and in the *Washington Observer-Reporter*.

Wendy Visser — Cambridge, Ontario — promotes the literary arts by public performance, teaching and speaking in schools, judging, and editing. Her work has been published in many anthologies including *In L.M.'s Garden* and *Writers Undercover* and the Herb Barrett Award haiku anthologies of 1998 and 1999.

f.ward (a.k.a. Frances Ward) — Hamilton, Ontario — was born in Manchester, England, but has lived in Hamilton for most of her adult life. Her poetry collections are *side effects*, *Life and Ledger*, and *The writer seems unaware....* She is the editor/publisher of *Hammered Out*. f.ward is a visual artist with many one-woman and group shows to her credit.

Liliane Welch — Sackville, New Brunswick — see page 176.

Patricia Wellingham-Jones — Tehama, California — is the author of 13 poetry titles: *Apple Blossoms at Eye Level*; *Bags*; *Big Day on the Ranch*; *California: Mountain & Stream Suite*; *Don't Turn Away: Poems About Breast Cancer*; *A Gathering Glance*; *Our Seventeen Years*; *Prune Harvest*; *SkyWords*; *Voices on the Land*; *Welcome, Babies*; *Wenonah: Growing Up in the '40s & '50s*; and *Words Unspoken*. She is also the editor/publisher of two anthologies, *Labyrinth: Prose & Poems* and *River Voices: Poets of Butte, Shasta, Tehama and Trinity Counties, California*. Patricia took first place in the *Midwest Poetry Review* Contest (for her poem "Flatlanders Head for the Hills," included in this volume) as well as the Reuben Rose International Poetry Prize (in Israel). Her website i www.snowcrest.net/pamelaj/wellinghamjones/home.htm

A.Z. Wells — Halifax, Nova Scotia — was born on Prince Edward Island and has lived in many places, including Montreal and seven years in the Canadian Arctic while employed by First Air. His collections are *Fool's Errand* and *Unsettled*. Zachariah's website is www.zachariahwells.com

Joanna M. Weston — Shawnigan Lake, British Columbia — was born in England and lived for many years in Prince Albert, Saskatchewan, before moving to B.C. She is the author of *One of These Little Ones, Cuernavaca Diary, Seasons, All Seasons,* and *The Willow-Tree Girl.* Like many poets, Joanna is a peace activist.

Patience Wheatley — Kingston, Ontario — was born and brought up in England, but moved to Montreal at the age of 15. She served in the Canadian army during World War II. Her three poetry collections are *A Hinge of Spring, Good-bye to the Sugar Refinery,* and *The Astrologer's Daughter.*

Sheila Windsor — Worcester, England — won the Annual Suruga Baika Award for her haiku "blustery morning," included in this volume. She has also received some 50 international awards for her haiku, tanka, renku, and linked haiku such as The James W. Hackett Award and the Kaji Aso Studio International Haiku Award. In addition to writing poetry, Sheila is a contemporary painter. Her website is
www.geocities.com/sheilaspaintings

Elana Wolff — Thornhill, Ontario — is the author of two poetry collections: *Birdheart* and *Mask.* She won second prize in the 2001 Orion Prize for Poetry contest as well as third prize in the 1999 Orion Prize for Poetry contest. She also won an honourable mention in the 1999 Milton Acorn Prize for Poetry contest and an honourable mention in the 2002 Tidepool Prize for Poetry contest. Her most recent success was first prize in the Tracking a Serial Poet Contest of *lichen* magazine. Elana contributes a monthly column to *Surface&Symbol.*

Margaret Malloch Zielinski — Ottawa, Ontario — won first prize in the 2000 Tidepool Prize for Poetry contest. She also won third prize (for her poem "Lizzie," included in this volume) as well as an honourable mention in the 2001 Milton Acorn Prize for Poetry contest. And she won third prize in the 2000 Milton Acorn Prize for Poetry contest and an honourable mention in the 2001 Orion Prize for Poetry contest. Margaret's first collection, *Driftwood,* was published in 2001. She was born in Scotland.

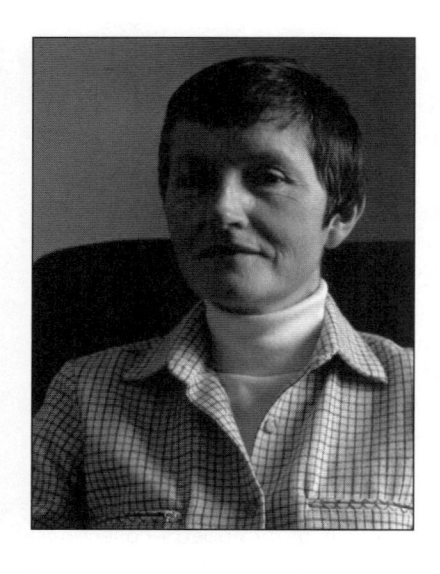

First prize winner
Liliane Welch

Poetry, the event of language *par excellence*, gives me the cues for all transports —for the good life. In this art form, all my occupations and loves are deepened; in it the restorative and challenging powers of nature and tradition are reconnected; through it I become alive to the present with all its refractions onto past and future, all insides and outsides.

The close attention and concentration, the celebration and gratitude required by poetry produce the miracle of the word; it is this that engulfs us, shapes us, and permits us to fly. When we take words into our hands, raise them up to the light, make them into carved stones, then they allow us to find our own voice and be the true custodians of our place.

Liliane Welch is the author of 20 collections of poems, most recently *Dispensing Grace*. She has co-authored two volumes of literary criticism on modern French poetry dealing with Baudelaire, Butor, Mallarmé, and Rimbaud. Her three books of essays are *Seismographs* (essays & memoirs), *Frescoes* (travel pieces), and *Untethered In Paradise* (essays on art). Her writings have been widely anthologized and translated into French, German, and Italian. Her many honours include the Bressani and Alfred Bailey Prizes. She is a *membre correspondant* of the Institut Grand Ducal of Luxembourg, her country of birth.

Her collections of poetry are *Winter Songs, Syntax of Ferment, Assailing Beats, October Winds, Brush and Trunks, From the Songs of the Artisans, Unrest Bound, Manstorna: Life on the Mountain, Word-House of a Grandchild, A Taste for Words, Fire to the Looms Below, Life in Another Language, Von Menschen und Orten, Dream Museum, Fidelities, Mosaics: Music Scapes Words, The Rock's Stillness, Unlearning Ice, This Numinous Bond*, and *Dispensing Grace*. With her husband Cyril, Liliane Welch makes her home in Sackville, New Brunswick.

Second prize winner
Roger Bell

Poetry is where you find it. It is there just waiting to be voiced. It may be the car accident where death slides in on oily wings or it may be the family of Baltimore orioles rioting through the crab apple tree on an early summer day. It takes only two things to write poetry: an ear that hears what is really being said or what might be said, and a love of language. Well, maybe a third thing: the patience to sit and observe and absorb, and to wait while the ear and the writerly tongue tussle to come up with what is right.

Roger Bell was born in 1949 and grew up in the wilds of Bruce County, Ontario. He currently lives in Port McNicoll, Ontario, within dreaming distance of Georgian Bay. Roger has been a high school teacher for 29 years. He is married and has two adult daughters. In 1997 he won the Shaunt Basmajian Chapbook Award for *Luke and the Wolf*. Roger was a finalist for the Milton Acorn Memorial People's Poetry Award in 1998 for *Real Lives*, and he has been a triple finalist for the CBC Literary Award. In addition to *Luke and the Wolf* and *Real Lives*, he is the author of *Mythtakes* and *When The Devil Calls*. He edited the anthology *Larger Than Life* and co-edited (with John B. Lee) *Henry's Creature — poems and stories on the automobile*.

Third prize winner
Marilyn Gear Pilling

When a poem comes to me, it's usually as a connection that happens in my mind, in the present. I go back in time to re-experience the smell, the texture, the taste, the look of the thing. This sets off in me a feeling, or perhaps an intuition. All this feels its way into words, feels its way onto the page. When writing a poem I am groping towards some kind of mystery. When my mind starts dolphin-leaping, that's when I'm happiest, because that means a poem is on the way.

The poet has her door open to the night world, the world of the unconscious, of dreams, of fantasy, of yin. Most occupations in our society take place in the day world, the world of logos—rules, order, hierarchy, intellect, logic. We need both kinds of knowledge to have a sane, balanced world, but our society values the logos kind of knowledge only, and has mostly closed the door to the knowledge that comes from dreams, from the dark, from the moon, the kind of knowledge that you will find in poetry.

I would say to people—if you are burnt out, if your inner world is a desert, poetry is where you might wish to look, for there you will find the water of life. Oases will spring up in the sands of your depletion and you will be revived. Poetry is the voice of the human soul.

> Marilyn Gear Pilling grew up in Waterloo (Ontario), but her roots are in Huron County. She is the author of two volumes of short fiction, *My Nose Is A Gherkin Pickle Gone Wrong* and *The Roseate Spoonbill of Happiness*. Her collection of poetry is *The Field Next To Love*. A retired librarian, she worked at the Hamilton Public Library for 31 years. She presently teaches in McMaster University's Continuing Education Department and serves on the executive of the Hamilton Poetry Centre. Marilyn has two grown daughters and lives in Hamilton with her husband.

Final Judge
Robert Sward

Robert Sward moved to Canada in 1969 to serve as Poet in Residence at the University of Victoria, founded a publishing house, Soft Press, and went on to work as book reviewer and feature writer for *The Globe and Mail* and the *Toronto Star*. He also produced four major broadcasts for the Canadian Broadcasting Corporation, including interviews with Margaret Atwood, Gwendolyn MacEwen, John Robert Colombo, Leonard Cohen, and Earle Birney. Over the years Robert has taught at Cornell University, the University of Iowa Writers' Workshop, and University of California, Santa Cruz Campus. Fulbright scholar at the University of Bristol and Guggenheim Fellow for Poetry, he was chosen by poet Lucille Clifton to receive a Villa Montalvo Literary Arts Award. Sward serves as contributing editor to *Web Del Sol, Alsop Review,* and *Blue Moon Review.*

Publications by Robert Sward
Poetry
Advertisements, 1958; *Uncle Dog & Other Poems*, 1962; *Kissing The Dancer & Other Poems*, 1964; *Thousand-Year-Old Fiancée*, 1965; *Horgbortom Stringbottom, I Am Yours, You Are History*, 1970; *Hannah's Cartoon*, 1970; *Quorum/Noah* (with Mike Doyle), 1970; *Gift*, 1971; *Five Iowa Poems*, 1975; *Cheers For Muktananda*, 1976; *Honey Bear On Lasqueti Island, B.C.*, 1978; *Six Poems*, 1980; *Twelve Poems*, 1982; *Movies: Left To Right*, 1983; *Half-A-Life's History, Poems New & Selected*, 1983; *The Three Roberts, Premiere Performance* (featuring Robert Priest, Robert Zend and Robert Sward), 1984; *The Three Roberts On Love*, 1985; *The Three Roberts On Childhood*, 1985; *Poet Santa Cruz*, 1985; *Four Incarnations, New & Selected Poems*, 1991; *Rosicrucian in the Basement*, 2001; *Three Dogs and a Parrot*, 2001; *Heavenly Sex, New & Selected Poems*, 2002; and *The Collected Poems, 1957-2004*, 2004.

Fiction
The Jurassic Shales (novel), 1975; *Family* (with contributions by David Swanger, Charles Atkinson, and Tilly Shaw), 1994; and *A Much-Married Man* (novel), 1996.

Non-Fiction
The Toronto Islands, An Illustrated History, 1983 and *Autobiography*, Contemporary Authors, Volume 206, 2003.

Audio CDs
(all recorded for the KPFA-FM Program "Cover to Cover," Berkeley, California)
Rosicrucian in the Basement, 2002; *Robert Sward: Poetry, Review & Interview* with Jack Foley, 2002; and *Writers' Friendship, Jack Foley and Robert Sward*, 2003.

Preliminary Judge
Bernadette Rule

Bernadette Rule was born and raised in the United States but moved to Canada many years ago. She currently lives in historic Fern Cottage in Dundas, Ontario. She is the author of five poetry collections, of which *Gardening at the Mouth of Hell* won the poetry prize of the Eden Mills Writers' Festival.

Bernadette teaches a course in writing non-fiction in McMaster University's writing program. In 1997 she edited *Remember me to Everybody: Letters from India, 1944 to 1949* by Frederick Gower Turnbull. She also works for the Separate School Board and serves on the Executive Board of the Hamilton Poetry Centre.

Poetry collections
Frames of Mind, 1985; *Full Light Falling*, 1988; *Private Places*, 1990; *Gardening at the Mouth of Hell*, 1996; and *The Weight of Flames*, 1998.

Acknowledgements

Roger Bell's "Shelby Springs Confederate Cemetery" and "Baby born in a toilet" are from his collection *When The Devil Calls*, Black Moss Press, 2000.

Paul Berry's "Remembering on GNER" was first published in *DIAL 174*.

Ronnie R. Brown's "Background Shadow" first appeared in *Arc* (Spring, 1991). "Family Ties" first appeared in *The Dalhousie Review* and later in her collection *Photographic Evidence*, Black Moss Press, 2000. "Pas de Deux" is from her collection *Re Creation*, Balmuir Poetry Series, 1987. "The Scent of Love" appeared in *Diviners* (Spring/Summer, 2000).

Anita Gevaudan Byerly's "Fourth and Hawkins — April, 1944" first appeared in the anthology *The Potter's Wheel*, Pittsburgh Poetry Society.

Gloe Cormie's "By the River on Opening Night" is from her collection *Sea Salt, Red Oven Mitts and the Blues* (2002).

Terrance Cox's "Armstrong's Cornet" is from his collection *Radio & Other Miracles*, Signature Editions, 2001.

Barbara Ruth Crupi's "Last Lines: The Letter" was first published in *Quantum Leap* (2000).

Fay Eagle's "Lot 109: Fanscape of a Victorian Lady" is from her collection *Journey into a Landscape*.

Rina Ferrarelli's "Y M Lee" was first published in *Pivot* and "On the Outer Banks" first appeared in *Dark Horse*.

Linda Frank's "You've Been on My Mind," "Turquoise," "November Rain," "Mercy," and "36°C" are from her collection *Cobalt Moon Embrace*, BuschekBooks, 2002.

Ann Goldring's haiku "above the branch" was first published by Haiku Canada in *small bird's small breath*.

Ellen S. Jaffe's "Chaco Canyon, Revisited" and "Night of My Conception: Ellen's Story, Out of the Ashes, June 1944" are from her collection *Water Children*, Mini Mocho Press, 2002.

Philomene Kocher's haiku "all the time now" first appeared in the anthology *beyond spring rain*, Haiku Canada, 2002.

Ken Kowal's "after the festival" is from his collection *Brookside Poems*, Highbrow Books, 2002.

John B. Lee's "Red Barns," "The Chair of Angels," "Walking Along Lake Erie," and "Paying Attention" are from his collection *The Half-Way Tree: poems selected and new, 1970-2000*, Black Moss Press, 2001.

John E. Marks' "Working Girls" is from his collection *Shelley*, poetryshack.

Sue Nevill's "azimuths" is from her collection *All You Expect of the Road*, Beach Holme Publishers, 2000.

Renee Norman's "My Father, Driving" first appeared in *The Amethyst Review* (Summer, 2002).

H.F. Noyes' three haiku are from his collection *still here*, Swamp Press, 2002.

Kathy Pearce-Lewis' "Aubade" is from the anthology *Rye Bread*, SCOP Publications.

Linda Vigen Phillips' "Dress Rehearsal" first appeared in *Procreation* (November, 1999).

Peggy Poole's "Fête de la Musique, Geneva" is from her collection *Polishing Pans*, Driftwood Publications, 2001.

Al Purdy's "House Guest" is a much-published poem. It most recently appeared in *Beyond Remembering: The Collected Poems of Al Purdy*, Harbour Publishing, 2000.

Gina Riley's "Bugbear" was first published in an Inklings anthology.

Lynn Veach Sadler's "As Silent as Mimes" was previously published in *Penumbra 1999* and *Urban Spaghetti* (1999).

Joanna Catherine Scott's "What Time Does" was published in the anthology *di-vêrsé-city*, Austin International Poetry Festival.

Shirley A. Serviss' "Sowing words" first appeared in the anthology *Our Fathers*, Rowan Books, 1995.

K.V. Skene's "In Like a Lion" is from her collection *Only a Dragon* (Canadian Poetry Association, Shaunt Basmajian Chapbook Award).

Tammara Or Slilat's "Atonement Day" was first published in the anthology *My Art Book*.

Jean Stanbury's "Tribute" is from her collection *Winged Seeds*, National Poetry Foundation, 1997.

Valerie Stetson's "Wedding Story Love" first appeared in *The Gaspereau Review*.

Sheila Stewart's "Ladybones" is from her collection *A Hat to Stop a Train*, Wolsak and Wynn Publishers, 2003.

Lynn Tait's "Mother and Son" was first published in *Quills* (Spring, 2004).

Carolyn Thomas's haiku "gathering creek stones" first appeared in *Young Leaves*, Yuki Teikei Haiku Society, 2000 and her "lake water" is from her collection *basho's frog*, Thinking Post Press, 1996.

Mildred Tremblay's "Codeine and Roses" is from her collection *Old Woman Comes Out of Her Cave*, Oolichan Books, 2001.

f.ward's "in spite of all those taxes" is from her collection *Life and Ledger*, Peter Street Publishing, 2002.

Liliane Welch's "Tattoo" was published in her collection *Fidelities,* Borealis Press, 1997. "Household Tools" was published in *Fidelities* and later in her collection *Untethered in Paradise*, Borealis Press, 2002. "Sex" and "Portage" are from her collection *The Rock's Stillness,* Borealis Press, 1999.

Patricia Wellingham-Jones's "Flatlanders Head for the Hills" first appeared in the *Midwest Poetry Review*, 2000.

Patience Wheatley's "In an Old Limestone House at Belleville" was first published in *Room of One's Own* (April, 1988) and was later included in her collection *Good-bye to the Sugar Refinery*, Goose Lane Editions, 1989.

Elana Wolff's "The Way to Make a Mask" is from her collection *Mask*, Guernica Editions, 2003.

Margaret Malloch Zielinski's "Lizzie" was first published in *After the Eclipse*, Mekler & Deahl, Publishers, 2004. Her "Mallory" first appeared in *Open Windows III*, Hidden Brook Press, 2002.

About Carl Sandburg

Carl Sandburg (1878–1967) worked at many jobs—day labourer, hobo, dishwasher, soldier, farm hand, and newspaper reporter — before publishing his first volume of poetry at the age of almost 40. His poetry titles include *Chicago Poems; Cornhuskers; Smoke and Steel; Slabs of the Sunburnt West; Good Morning, America; The People, Yes; Honey and Salt; Breathing Tokens; Billy Sunday and Other Poems;* and *Poems for the People.* Sandburg twice won the Pulitzer Prize for poetry. He won a third Pulitzer for his history of Abraham Lincoln's Civil War years. All told, more than 30 books of poetry, fiction, non-fiction, and children's literature bear his name.

In addition to his work for daily newspapers in Chicago, Sandburg also wrote for the *International Socialist Review* and *The Masses*. He founded what Selden Rodman called Proletarian Poetry (now better known as Populist Poetry) and inspired many of the poets who came onto the American scene during the 1930s, such as Muriel Rukeyser, Kenneth Fearing, and the Benét brothers.

A realist who always had a broad romantic streak, Sandburg never surrendered his faith in the basic goodness of the People. His poetry was therefore noted for its rock-hard strength as well as its drifting-fog tenderness. At the time of his death he was America's favourite poet.

About Dorothy Livesay

Dorothy Livesay (1909–1996) had a remarkable seventy-year literary career. Livesay was a leading People's Poet, literary editor, magazine publisher, mentor, feminist, and social justice activist. She was one of the first poets in Canada to write about Marxism, the lives of working people, and women's sexuality. She also took on the taboo subject of aging as she herself grew older. In fact, there was no subject Livesay was afraid to tackle. While she was still an undergraduate at the University of Toronto, Livesay took on campus sexism and the academic establishment. And while active in the League of Canadian Poets she took on professional and academic elitism. She was a supporter of gay and lesbian rights when almost no one else was.

With her third and fourth books—*Day and Night* (1944) and *Poems for People* (1947), both Governor General's Award winners — she set the tone for People's Poetry in Canada. Indeed, much of the poetry written during the 1950s, '60s, and '70s was inspired by her example. Livesay's influence can be seen in the work of such poets as Margaret Atwood, Milton Acorn, and Rhea Tregebov. Her selected poems, *The Self-Completing Tree*, is a definitive work. An overview of her life work is presented in the posthumous *Archive for Our Times*. Her strong words and stronger deeds are missed by all who love Canadian poetry.

Other Books by Unfinished Monument Press / hamilton haiku press / Mekler & Deahl, Publishers

Poetry
Milton Acorn, *To Hear the Faint Bells:*
  haiku, senryu and short poems from Canada's national poet
Milton Acorn & James Deahl, *A Stand of Jackpine*
Milton Acorn & Cedric Smith, *The Road to Charlottetown*
Becky D. Alexander (editor), *Paradise Poems: haiku from Cootes Paradise*
Herb Barrett, *The Light Between*
Fred Cogswell (editor), *Doors of the Morning*: The 1996 Sandburg-Livesay Award
James Deahl, *Blackbirds*
James Deahl (editor), *Mix Six*
James Deahl (editor), *The Northern Red Oak: poems for and about Milton Acorn*
James Deahl, *When Rivers Speak*
Chris Faiers and Mark McCawley (editors), *Small Press Lynx:*
  An Anthology of Small Press Writers
Simon Frank, *Imaginary Poems*
LeRoy Gorman (editor), *Gathering Light*: The 1996 Herb Barrett Award
Albert W.J. Harper, *Poems of Reflection*
Hans Jongman (editor), *Sweeping Leaves:* the 1999 Herb Barrett Award
John B. Lee, *The Echo of Your Words Has Reached Me*
Tanis MacDonald, *This Speaking Plant*: The 1996 Acorn-Rukeyser Award
Joy Hewitt Mann, *grass*: The 1999 Acorn-Rukeyser Award
Judge Mazebedi, *Chicken Cries Out*
Walt Peterson, *In the Waiting Room of the Speedy Muffler King:*
  The 1998 Acorn-Rukeyser Award
Ted Plantos (editor), *Not to Rest in Silence: A celebration of people's poetry*
Poetry Forever, *After the Eclipse*
Al Purdy (judge), *Sing for the Inner Ear*: The 1997 Sandburg-Livesay Award
Kay Redhead, *The Song of the Artichoke Lover*
Linda Rogers, *Picking the Stones*: The 1997 Acorn-Rukeyser Award
Margaret Saunders (editor), *Cold Morning*: The 1997 Herb Barrett Award
Joanna C. Scott, *Coming Down from Bataan*: The 2000 Acorn-Rukeyser Award
Jeff Seffinga, *Bailey's Mill*
Jeff Seffinga (editor), *A Cliff Runs Through It*
Jeff Seffinga (editor), *Ingots*
Jeff Seffinga, *Tight Shorts: haiku and other short poems*
Raymond Souster (judge), *No Choice but to Trust*: The 1999 Sandburg-Livesay Award
Michael Dylan Welch (editor), *Through the Spirea*: The 1998 Herb Barrett Award
Jim C. Wilson (judge), *Waiting for You to Speak*: The 1998 Sandburg-Livesay Award

Non-fiction
Terry Barker, *After Acorn: A Meditation on Canada's People's Poet*
David Allen Greene, *The Script of Under the Watchful Eye*
Claire Ridker & Patricia Savage, *Railing Against the Rush of Years:*
  A personal journey through aging via art therapy

Note: The Sandburg-Livesay Anthology Contest has been discontinued, as have the Acorn-Rukeyser Chapbook Contest and the Herb Barrett Award.

The Sandburg-Livesay Award

1996 Elinor Benedict, co-winner
Carol Rose, co-winner

1997 Ronnie R. Brown, First
Joan Woodcock, Second

1998 Peggy Poole, First
Gillian Harding-Russell, Second

1999 Sandee Gertz Umbach, First
Rina Ferrarelli, Second
Joy Hewitt Mann, Third

2000 Liliane Welch, First
Roger Bell, Second
Marilyn Gear Pilling, Third